THE 20-MINUTE
NETWORKING MEETING

Executive Edition

The
20-Minute
Networking
Meeting

EXECUTIVE EDITION

Learn to Network. Get a Job.

MARCIA BALLINGER, PHD
and NATHAN A. PEREZ

CAREER INNOVATIONS PRESS

**Volume book orders are available at a discount.
Contact Career Innovations Press for more information.
www.20mnm.com**

Published 2012 by Career Innovations Press.
Cover design by Linda Koutsky
Interior design by Linda Koutsky

ISBN: 978-0-9859106-0-0
Ebook ISBN: 978-0-9859106-1-7

*Marcia would like to dedicate this book to
her husband, Brad, and daughter, Analisa.*

* * *

*Nathan would like to dedicate this book to his wife, Jessica.
Thank you for your patience and belief.*

Contents

APPENDIX

ABOUT THE AUTHORS

Acknowledgments

The *20-Minute Networking Meeting* is rooted in two core values: Collaboration and Community. We believe that a successful organization (and a successful individual!) needs to care about a wide variety of constituencies and stakeholders and to treat each with concern and respect.

One way that Collaboration and Community come into play is in the networking we, as recruitment professionals, do with people in job transition. Even when we are not working on a related search, we seek to assist each person who contacts us by sharing information with them, offering helpful suggestions, or perhaps, giving a word of encouragement.

We would like to acknowledge the wisdom and generosity of Rebecca Driscoll, Mike Frommelt, Lars Leafblad, Diane Meskan, Adreanne Peters, Lisa Curtin, and Bob Schoenbaum. Two of our esteemed colleagues in the executive search industry, Carla Anderson and David Magy, provided valuable insights. Experienced leaders in our Executives group offered perspectives on the challenges of networking while in a job transition. Many of these executives were willing to spend time with us, either over the phone or in person, in order for us to hear their stories.

We would like to offer them our heartfelt thanks.

We would also like to recognize the outstanding work being done to help executives manage through career transitions—in particular, we especially would like to thank our partners at Navigate Forward, Inc.; Career Partners International, Twin Cities; Challenger, Gray & Christmas, Inc.; Cultivating Careers; George Dow Consulting, LLC.; Lee Hecht Harrison; Right Management; The Prouty Project and The Bailey Group, who do phenomenal work with senior executives, boards, and organizations; and to Mark Richards, an expert networker who truly "gets it."

Finally, as writing a book is seldom a single-person effort, we'd like to recognize and thank our editor, Ben Barnhart. His conceptual insights and help have been invaluable in getting our book published. Thanks is also due to our copy editor, Carolyn Berge, for her eagle eye. Last, but not least, an important debt of gratitude is owed to both Stuart M. Perelmuter for his expert coverage and availability through the entire writing and editing process, and to Bruce Schneier for his early impressions of *The 20-Minute Networking Meeting* manuscript.

Thank you to all.

THE 20-MINUTE
NETWORKING MEETING

Executive Edition

Introduction

Welcome to *The 20-Minute Networking Meeting!* The information contained in this book *will* revolutionize the way you think about networking, whether you're in transition or a working executive looking to proactively manage your career by honing your networking skills. Meeting with job-seeking executives like you every day, I've observed what works in networking—from the other side of the desk. Subsequently, I've also observed what does *not* work, and, sadly, what I've found is that the vast majority of networking meetings are near-complete failures. *The 20-Minute Networking Meeting* is meant to remedy that.

The objective in writing this book is to show you what networking looks like from your contacts' perspective. It is my hope that you will learn to conduct meetings that those contacts will find valuable, engaging, and impressive—in less than twenty minutes. The material in this book is designed with *you* in mind. *Everything* in it is relevant to your situation as a networking executive. So don't skip ahead. Having a full understanding of the model is imperative to your success. But if that isn't enough to convince you, then allow me to say the information contained herein will affect much more than just getting your next job. It will affect the rest of your career.

Let's get on with it.

PART ONE

A Couple of
Networking Stories . . .

Doreen & Paul

Doreen looked at her calendar. A day full of meetings! The first one, she noted, was a networking meeting with Paul Samuelson, a former coworker. He had contacted her a couple of weeks ago, shared that he was in a job transition, and asked for some of her time to reconnect as part of his job search.

Of course, Doreen had said yes. Her cousin had gone through a job transition a few years ago, and she knew how tough it could be. There were no available jobs for Paul at HGW, Doreen's current company. But Paul had led a great engineering function that supported her former business unit, and she felt confident that he had something to offer someone in her network.

When the receptionist called to let Doreen know that Paul had arrived, she grabbed a notebook and headed to the lobby. As she walked by her boss's office, he called out and asked if she could join an executive team conference call in an hour. It was important, he said.

"Sure!" she said, knowing that her boss did not convene the group at the drop of a hat for no reason. She had to be there.

In the lobby, Doreen greeted Paul warmly. It was great to see him after so much time. With her unscheduled call looming, she quickly led him to a conference room to get things started.

On the way, Doreen asked Paul about some mutual acquaintances and about his family. Of course, given how much time had passed, Paul had a lot of updates. As they sat and got settled, he reminisced about some of their former colleagues, and asked if she could remember others who were outside of her unit. She could recall only some.

Over Paul's shoulder, Doreen glanced at the clock. She had started their conversation, but didn't feel comfortable stepping on his toes to get back on track. But they had already chatted for ten minutes, and she knew that she needed some time to prep for that call.

Taking advantage of a lull, she smiled, opened her notebook, and asked outright:

"So, what can I do, Paul? Tell me how I can help." He was a good guy and colleague, and her offer was genuine.

Paul cleared his throat and looked at the notebook in his lap. It was evident from the get-go that his transition was taking a toll on him. His face fell, and his earlier enthusiasm nearly vanished.

"Okay, so . . ." he started, and then he commenced to give her some background as to what happened.

It was a tough story. A long story. An uncommon tale of corporate takeover. He expressed how poorly he felt he'd been treated when he was laid off, but he didn't seem to be doing much better now than when it occurred months before. Hoping to help her understand the experience, Paul even shared what she guessed had to be confidential details about his boss and the company's performance. That thought concerned her. She wondered if any of her HGW colleagues had left and had these types of conversations.

She didn't think it was very wise.

Another glance over Paul's shoulder showed that time was dwindling fast. Paul hadn't even mentioned what type of position he was seeking now.

"Well, let me tell you about my background," he said when she asked.

Doreen wasn't in time to stop him, and she cared too much about interrupting her friend to ask for an abbreviated version. But he was already giving her the long version of his résumé. There was a lot of detail. Too much detail. More than anyone else had offered at one time, and it was eating into their networking opportunity.

Paul finally finished, and then he asked, "Could you tell me more about what you guys do here at HGW?"

Doreen blinked. Did he not already know? Had he not looked at the website?

"No, I didn't," Paul chuckled. "I was just so busy. Figured you could tell me as we caught up."

Another glance at the clock. She knew she had to hurry this meeting if she was going to give Paul any helpful information. But then she realized she shouldn't be running this meeting at all.

Still, Doreen gave a high-level summary of her company's products and markets. As she did, she couldn't help recalling how Paul used to be such a well-prepared executive. Now he asked questions as she spoke, but Doreen just couldn't understand what his questions had to do with his job search.

There was a knock on the conference room window. It was her boss, indicating they would be starting the call soon.

Doreen felt terrible about ending the meeting, and Paul looked disappointed.

"I guess we kind of ran long, huh?" he said with a smile. He started to speak quickly. "Well, any help you can give me . . ."

Doreen wished that he would offer her some direction. But she was forced to take the lead again when he trailed off.

"I'm not sure yet what you're looking for, but unfortunately we don't have any openings here at HGW at the moment."

Paul tapped on his still-unopened notebook.

"Do you know of any other companies with job openings for a VP of engineering? I mean, since you're working, maybe you have your ear to the ground?"

She shook her head. Knowing such things wasn't part of her day-to-day practice, and she wasn't connected in engineering circles anymore.

There was an awkward silence, but this time she didn't know how to fill it. She had fully intended to help, but he had given her nothing to go on, and she was about to send him away with nothing.

I have some suggestions of other people he might contact, she thought. But he doesn't seem prepared enough to meet them. Besides, she wasn't sure she wanted to endorse him at this time anyway. He didn't seem to know what he was looking for.

"Well, we should at least stay in touch," Doreen proposed, standing up. "I'll let you know right away if something comes up."

He grinned at her. He clearly understood that this meeting hadn't turned out the way either of them had intended. He held out his hand.

"It was great to see you again," Paul said as she shook his hand. "And yes, please do keep me in mind."

He grabbed his things, and she walked him to the reception area. On the way out, she glanced at the clock once more. Fifty-nine minutes with Paul Samuelson, and while they'd caught up some, they'd accomplished nothing. She felt horrible. Worse, Paul hadn't said thank you once.

And now let's take a look at a networking meeting that went a little differently.

Jon & Suzanne

Jon dropped into his chair and snapped up his calendar. With the end of tax season coming, he was finally seeing the light at the end of the tunnel. At the same time, it was getting busier than ever as the April 15 deadline approached. On his to-do list today: Pluck out more of his clients' W2s from an eight-inch stack of mail and return at least a dozen calls before five. Then there was email. And daily review meetings to prep for.

His phone rang. Jon dropped the calendar and picked up the handset.

"Jon Carlsson," he answered far more relaxed than he felt.

"Jon, it's Suzanne. I'm at the Starbucks down the street and thought I'd bring you a coffee for our nine o'clock meeting."

Jon sat up and grabbed the calendar again. Suzanne? Her name was there, but her face was missing from his mind. Had he made this appointment?

"Jon, did I lose you?"

"A latte would be fantastic; thank you for offering," he responded, still in a relaxed tone. If she was polite enough to offer, he would be polite enough to accept. But he gritted his teeth. How had this happened? How had he scheduled something in the busiest time of year?

"Latte it is," Suzanne said. "See you in a few minutes."

Ten minutes later, Jon showed her into his office, closing the door behind them. Her name was ringing a bell now, but he was still wracking his brain to place her face. He felt terrible that he would have to admit this. Worse, he didn't know if he could commit to an hour for an unplanned meeting.

"Thank you again for taking the time to meet, Jon," Suzanne said as she placed her folio on the table. "I know you're in your busy season, so I won't keep you long."

Jon sat across from her with a tense smile.

"Just a reminder as to our connection," Suzanne continued, settling herself in. "Molly Lin, who sends her hellos, suggested I reach out to you. It was quite a few weeks ago. She warned that you were about to hit tax season, but she insisted that we might be able to help each other network. So, thank you, again, for your time."

Molly! thought Jon, letting out a subtle sigh of relief. It finally all came back to him now. Suzanne was a friend of Molly's, Jon's former business partner. He knew he wouldn't have scheduled this if it wasn't important. But now that he realized it was a networking meeting, he wished he could have put it off till after the 15th. He could hear the emails rolling in behind Suzanne even as he sat there. And the red light on his phone flashed at him as she spoke.

"But even though we're networking," Suzanne went on as though reading his mind, "I'll only take twenty minutes of your time."

Twenty minutes. He'd heard that before. What she meant was an hour, and he didn't have that. He glanced at the clock again. Their meeting had to start *now*.

"Here is my situation," Suzanne said, one step ahead. She opened her folio. "It's a fairly common story these days: I was caught up in a downsizing at Holt Company. I know you don't have job openings here for me, but I just really value the chance to make contact and discuss a thing or two."

Joseph, Jon's assistant, poked his nose in the door.

"A reminder about your ten o'clock review meeting," he said, putting a stack of material on Jon's desk. "They're coming to your office."

The review meeting! That was pushed up to today and was less than an hour away. If his meeting with Suzanne was like any other, he wouldn't be prepared.

Joseph left the room. The door clicked closed.

"No problem with time, Jon," Suzanne said, reading his mind again. "I promised—only twenty minutes."

Suzanne jumped right back in.

"Molly and I were both accounting majors. She went into public accounting, where, as you know, she has had a stellar career. I think I mentioned that I just spoke with her last week, and she sends you her best. I, on the other hand, joined my dad's company, a foundry, as staff accountant. Later, I became the controller for the organization and worked closely with my father as we expanded our operations. When my father became ill, we decided to seriously look at selling the company, which we did, five years ago. Since then, I've been at Holt, first as a division controller, and recently as their corporate audit director. With the changes that you've no doubt read about in our company, several positions were eliminated, mine included."

Suzanne's demeanor was steady. She didn't come off as negative or apologetic, given her circumstances. Jon admired her attitude; being out of work was not easy. He knew by experience.

"So," she continued. "I now have nearly twenty years of experience in finance and accounting, mostly in small and mid-size organizations. And while I think I'd like to find a similar role, I'd like to focus my questions for you on your perceptions of some possible career directions."

Jon hesitated. He wasn't sure he was the right person to give answers on career direction.

Again, Suzanne seemed to read his thoughts.

"I've been asking several people these same questions. Different perspectives are important, and I would really value your thoughts." He glanced at the clock again. He was sure this is where things would get out of hand, but he gave her the benefit of the doubt anyway. She seemed to have a handle on what she wanted out of the meeting.

"Sure," Jon said. "Fire away."

Moving right along, Suzanne asked Jon about growth areas that he was seeing with his clients. The recent several weeks had given Jon plenty to talk about in terms of trends in his industry, and he shared the high points over the next ten minutes or so. As he did, Suzanne busily scribbled notes in her notebook, asking pertinent questions along the way. He grinned pleasantly in spite of being stressed about time. She was actually taking him seriously, and asking questions about subjects that he could talk about.

After he finished his last thought, Suzanne tapped her pen on her notebook thoughtfully.

"You've actually answered my other questions," she smiled. "Also, if you don't mind sharing—who else would you suggest I connect with as part of my networking?"

He'd been asked this before. Usually it was uncomfortable giving out names, but Suzanne seemed to have her act together. She clearly knew what she was talking about and she showed her gratitude for being there. Now he understood why Molly had insisted Suzanne reach out, and he didn't hesitate to give her a name.

"Lenny Ditzliv," he said. Lenny was a good referral, and Jon knew Lenny would appreciate Suzanne's sharp and together attitude. "He's retiring in a few years, but he seems to know everyone in financial circles in the north part of the city. Go ahead and use my name. He's an old friend and long-term client."

Suzanne wrote down the information and smiled. Without taking any more time, she closed her folio and put away her pen.

"Thanks so much, Jon. Your time was very helpful. As I said at the beginning of our meeting, I want to be sensitive of your schedule." She gathered her things into a neat pile, stopped, and folded her hands. "But one last question: How can I be helpful to *you*?"

Jon was taken aback. What job seeker asks a question like this?

"Um . . . I can't think of anything at the moment . . ."

"The company that purchased my father's company is called Allbright & Daly. I would be very happy to introduce you to their top financial executive if you think that would be beneficial. I'm sure they'd be glad to know of a terrific accounting firm."

He found himself smiling again. That was extremely thoughtful, and he'd long wanted to connect with that firm.

"That would be wonderful. Thank you."

She smiled and stood up, extending her hand. He shook it.

"Thank you again, Jon," she said. "It was a pleasure to meet you."

He walked her to the door, and a quick glance at the clock showed that he still had over a half hour to prepare for the review meeting. She had actually stuck to twenty minutes.

"I'll be sure to tell Molly hello for you once I let her know we had a chance to meet," Suzanne said. "Have a great rest of the week."

"Thank you, Suzanne. And thank you, again, for the coffee."

This Book Is for *You*

You could probably relate to some part of the previous two stories. As you saw, some networking meetings are just a little smoother (not to mention more successful) than others. But it's not just chance or luck that determines whether a meeting goes well. It's skill—skill that can be learned and perfected with practice. This book will break down the successful networking meeting into its essential parts, and give you the tools needed to make your networking meetings successful. Before that, though, here is bit of necessary background on how the model was built.

I'm a principal and co-founder of a prominent, Minneapolis-based, retained executive search firm. My colleagues and I are contacted literally every day by professionals seeking to network with us as part of their job search. It's a sensible part of an executive's job-search strategy, but we have come to dread this oft-repeated request, regardless of how much we appreciate meeting these bright individuals.

"Hello. This is Susan SuperExec. I was referred to you because I'm looking for a new job. I'm networking, and I want to meet with you."

Why do we dread these meetings when these talented professionals are our bread and butter? Because the meetings are almost always ineffective. In fact, some are *so* ineffective that it would have been better if the job seeker had not called at all. And other meetings, while adequate enough, simply miss their full potential.

Over time, I began to see what was consistently going wrong. I took notes. On occasion, I also saw what was going right. I took more notes. What I ultimately observed was that the foundation of the networking meeting was being overlooked entirely. Potentially terrific networking meetings were suffering a fatal blow. Those meetings were not well planned, well run, or even meaningful. They *certainly* didn't have mutuality or gratitude.

I shared these notes with my peers—people who are also frequently asked to network—and they overwhelmingly agreed that most networking meetings are entirely too long, problematic, and ineffective. Thus, *The 20-Minute Networking Meeting.*

The 20-Minute Networking Meeting is written from a hiring and recruiting perspective, and it will tell you what works for the people you are contacting and hoping to impress. Step-by-step, we will analyze the structure of successful networking meetings and show you how you can put this model to work for you.

Before we dig into the model of *The 20-Minute Networking Meeting*, let's take a look at why networking is so crucial for executives in job transition.

Why Networking
Is So Important

(Or: Hey, Friend, Your Job Market Is Hiding from You)

Perhaps you haven't given this a lot of thought, but experienced executives in transition can have a distinct disadvantage next to other job seekers. Why? Because for the majority of executives, these roles are not filled by online résumé databases or community job boards.

So, where *does* one find these jobs? Well, in the *invisible* job market, of course!

You have undoubtedly heard of it before, and, yes, it does exist. The invisible job market consists of job openings that are not advertised or publicly announced. These positions are filled by (or sometimes created for) candidates who come to an employer's attention through employee recommendations, referrals from trusted associates, recruiters, or direct contact with the candidates who may be interviewing for these jobs.

And where would this invisible job market be?

You're standing in it. It's all around you, all the time. It's there when you pick up your phone and when you send an email. In fact, it's the very rumor that you've *heard* before even reading about it.

So how do you become a part of it?

Occasionally through executive recruiters like us. Or the magic portal into the Invisible Dimension. That one's hard to find, though, so networking is your better bet.

Networking, you say with a grimace. ***Does it really come down to networking?***

Yes, it does. But the good news is it's easier than you think. Networking, to the casual practitioner, is all about who you know, rather than what you know. And while there's truth to that, it doesn't tell the whole story. The reality is if you haven't developed networking skills, then who you know simply won't matter. In fact, undeveloped networking skills will be the leading cause of closed doors and unanswered calls. But build those skills, and networking will provide you the exact opposite experience. Which is why you're reading this book. Learn the skill set contained herein, and you'll be adding valuable contacts and useful information that will take you anywhere you want to go.

What kind of useful information? A clearer understanding of what your market is looking for and where you fit in that market are a couple of examples.

◇◇

POTENTIAL NETWORKING CONTACTS

- Former co-workers, peers, and staff from your previous employer
- Vendors, suppliers, and clients you've worked with
- Professional colleagues, such as folks you've met at trade associations, conferences, or training programs

- Consultants you've hired
- Fellow alumni from the college(s) you attended
- Fellow members of boards or civic and athletic clubs
- Friends, neighbors, and members of your faith community
- Professional service providers, such as your accountant, attorney, and tax preparer

◇◇◇

Important Note: The boxed examples are only meant to be a "jump start" in building your contact base. There is no limit to how wide your network can grow. You'll keep adding new names to your network as you meet new people.

Also, don't forget that there are many networking groups specifically for executives in transition. Fellow members of these groups, in addition to being sources of ideas and moral support, can also be potential networking contacts themselves!

What It is, What It Does, and Why It Works

Perhaps the answers to these questions are already obvious to you, but if they're not, let's cut to the heart of it. For our purposes we're going to focus on networking as it relates to job seekers. If you're in job transition, this next statement sums up the importance of establishing a vibrant network:

A CEO isn't going to hire you if he or she doesn't *know* you. Right? Right.

But your chances increase tenfold if you've at least been introduced to that CEO by a colleague, friend, or neighbor.

If you know one person, and that person knows another, you have a valid and working (however small) network. Imagine if your network included dozens of people. Or hundreds. With a network this large, you could certainly achieve your goals. You would surely find out about the invisible job market. And there's no doubt you'd find out who's hiring.

And that's networking. If you still have reservations or doubts, I can tell you firsthand that I see it work for executives every day. Additionally, I see it work right here in my office. One of my colleagues has been voted the Most Networked Person in the Twin Cities, while the co-author of this book, Nathan, expands his LinkedIn network by roughly 800 to 900 people per month and has been cited as one of the Huffington Post's most linked people on LinkedIn, worldwide.

Now let's dig a bit deeper.

Loosely defined, networking is the practice of meeting with other people with a specific purpose in mind. (In your case, it would be to find your terrific next job.) I've mentioned that this practice is imperative at the executive and professional levels. Simply put (and back to basics again), people have to know who you are. Personally. There is no biography or work history (résumé) that's going to get the job (hunt) done faster.

So, besides networking, what are the other ways to go about getting executive work?

Well, there are job boards, advertisements, online applications, mailed inquiries, and ringing doorbells. But let's be honest here. When was the last time you saw a job posting for an executive-level position in the classifieds?

Right. Not likely. You simply can't and won't hear about executive opportunities in papers or on job boards. And though you might find something out there on the information-drenched World Wide Web, it's probably going to be a sore discovery when you realize that it's not in your field or even something you're interested in.

But for the sake of argument, let's say you do find something. Can you imagine the hundreds of other applicants you'd be competing with just to be looked at? It suddenly makes the idea of finding a magic portal a little more appealing, doesn't it?

Which takes us back to networking.

Conventional wisdom, if you haven't already heard it ad nauseam, says that eighty percent of all executive jobs are "listed" on the invisible job market. From our perspective this is true. Therefore, eighty percent of your job search should be directed toward face-to-face activities. Résumés and application submissions often end up in a queue, if not a recycle pile, and that will do you no good. So what must be done? You must get on your feet.

◇◇◇

> All résumés must be sifted and studied. There are piles, there are those who sift through piles. Face-to-face meetings are the way to cut to through the competition. Efficient, to the point, with contact. *Then* will you be visible in the invisible job market.

◇◇◇

The good news is that you *already* have a network. Every person you know is in it. Better yet, every person you meet expands it. Professional trade groups are a great place to get things moving. Seminars and functions geared toward networking are even better; there's no better place to hone your skills before getting into the Important Stuff.

But wait, wait, you say. If eighty percent of my search work should be face-to-face meetings, what about the other twenty percent of my time?

Glad you asked. If you must use the web for your job search, then I would suggest using your twenty percent searching those online postings. But an even better idea would be to use that time to correspond via email and follow up with brief thank-yous for those completed face-to-face meetings.

How Networking (*Really*) Works

As we've mentioned already, executive-level jobs are typically filled by contacts that come from personal relationships. Whether intentional or not, it's the common approach in business. For instance, a strong recommendation from a trusted source could be all that's needed for you to get an interview with a CEO. (Decision makers look to their networks for valued suggestions and referrals. There's no way someone can *know* a candidate by reading a piece of paper outlining a work history, so their contacts' trusted word is paramount.) As an example, when a search starts, the first question a hiring decision maker usually asks is:

"Hey—who do you know that can do this job?"

The answer, more often than not, is:

"Let me think about whom I know."

And *justlikethat*, the networking has begun. Don't you want to be the person who comes to mind right away?

Here's a scenario. Let's presume there are two potential candidates with similar backgrounds. We'll call them Passive Candidate and Active Candidate. They are both in job transition, having been laid off on the same day, and both are networking for similar jobs in the same city. Essentially, they're in the exact same scenario.

Passive Candidate has been slow to start the networking process, focusing instead on combing the Internet and studying online postings. He's comfortable taking it easy, and using this methodology, he's set up a few networking meetings.

Active Candidate has put her time toward active networking. By phoning some former colleagues, sending out emails to past clients, and scheduling lunches with several employed friends, Active Candidate 'succeeds in conducting twenty-five networking meetings. (Remember—*anyone* you know is in your network. And as one never knows who holds key information to your job search, your contact base can easily add up to twenty-five or more people.) Active Candidate and Passive Candidate are quickly on two different paths.

Just to make things interesting, though, let's say that Active Candidate didn't feel too hot about the result of some of her meetings. (We'll come back to this in a minute.)

Okay, so far we have two people, same set of cards, two different approaches, and a number of meetings. Now let's develop the invisible job market.

Switch to the perspective of the CEO who is looking to fill a new role. He has talked to those around him about the position—"Hey, who do you know that can do this job?"—and word has begun to spread through his trusted network of peers, former colleagues, and personal friends. As it does, those people share this information with their network of peers, former colleagues, and personal friends, letting them know that a new executive role is up for grabs at ABC Company.

Voilà! A posting on the invisible job market exists.

With all the pieces on the table, it should be clear that Active Candidate has the edge. But let's look more closely at how she gained that edge.

If any of those twenty-five people whom Active Candidate happened to meet with is in the extended network of the CEO, Active Candidate's going to hear word of the opportunity. Plain and simple. To be more specific, people talk, and people pass forward this kind of information. With each new person who learns of this new job, it can be surmised that the information will be disseminated to at least one, if not a few, more people, and so on until there is a widely cast net. Active Candidate will hear of the opportunity, *just by being in the network.*

Passive Candidate, on the other hand, likely doesn't even know the job exists yet. Why? It's less likely that Passive Candidate's network overlaps with the CEO's extended network (yes, it's *possible*, just less likely). So, without actively growing his network, Passive Candidate is letting this opportunity pass him by. What's more, this job isn't likely posted online, and the only way to hear about it is by being part of the network that's connected to the invisible job market.

It should now be crystal clear how Active Candidate stands a pretty good chance of getting a face-to-face meeting with ABC Company. Agreed?

Now let's go back to Active Candidate's not-so-good meeting that we mentioned earlier, just so we can draw another networking point.

Let's just say, for sake of our networking argument, that word from the CEO has finally made its way down the grapevine to one of the people that Active Candidate met with. But for some reason that meeting didn't go well. Maybe it was bumpy, maybe someone was tired, or maybe the contact was somewhat reluctant to meet in the first place. (Sometimes we have bad days.) Even if this were the case, Active Candidate has become an extension of the total network anyway. She immediately becomes the first qualified person to pop into her contact's head, bumpy meeting or not. That alone makes her *far* more likely to get the job than Passive Candidate, who is still at home basking in the glow of his computer screen. Wouldn't you say?

And *justlikethat*, Active Candidate has become visible in the invisible job market. Passive Candidate, on the other hand, simply wouldn't know any better.

Becoming the Best (Networker) You Can Be

I've alluded to the fact that I'm a frequent recipient of requests for networking meetings from executives in job transition. Why me? Well, primarily because I work in executive search, an industry that is chock-full of bright minds and savvy business-doing. The nature of our work also sees us working with company decision makers when filling roles. Consequently, executive recruiters are highly sought-after networking targets, and we get lots of calls. There is a strong perception that executive recruiters have "secret caches" of highly desirable jobs hidden in their jacket pockets. That's not true, of course, but the perception is there. The truth is that the only jobs I have at any given moment are the jobs that our clients—the companies that retain us to fill executive openings—have hired us to help fill.

So, even though executive recruiters are not likely to have a specific opportunity for a job-seeking executive at the moment he or she calls, we are still seen as highly desirable networking contacts. We know people. We know the job market.

I think another reason that I get so many networking requests is that I have a reputation for saying yes. I'm known as a recruiter who will take your call, chat with you on the phone, and frequently agree to meet with you in person. I have heard countless networkers tell me that I have a reputation for being "nice" and "helpful."

Regardless of the reasons, I end up with lots of networking meetings; certainly well over a thousand so far in my career.

I don't just participate in individual networking meetings. A few years ago, I started consolidating some of my networking meetings into monthly group sessions called "Keystone Coffee," where I invite several executives in transition to network with me in a roundtable, Q&A format. In addition, I speak frequently to large groups of executives in transition, in a variety of settings.

Earlier, I stated that most of the networking meetings I participate in are ineffective. If you've networked with me recently, I mean no offense. But it's true. From my side of the desk, most job seekers conduct their networking meetings poorly.

Many executives in job transition focus a lot of their attention on résumés and LinkedIn profiles—how to write them, how to format them, how to make sure that keywords are highlighted, and how often to send or share them. By contrast, they don't think much about their face-to-face meetings— the *one* thing that gets jobs! And yet, from an executive recruiter's perspective (not just mine, mind you), networking is where the major problems are. And, networking is where the opportunities lie.

You can tweak your résumé from here to kingdom come and it might not make any difference. It will not likely help you stand out from the pack. How perfectly written does it need be? How many résumés do you need to send out to get even one response? How many databases do you need to be in?

But, what if you were to become an expert networker? Someone who is well regarded by a large group of connections? Someone for whom each interaction is a job-seeking home run?

Someone who has a broad network that is actively engaged in helping you find your next great job? An expert networker?

Now we're talking!

Using *The 20-Minute Networking Meeting* model, you will find yourself conducting brief, powerful meetings that quickly expand your network and begin to establish your name in the invisible job market. As an executive, you already know much of this information. It's just a matter of putting it into practice in a way that you and your networking contacts will find efficient and mutually beneficial.

I want to show you how to accomplish the fundamental tasks of any executive in a job transition:

- Gather new information
- Add new contacts to your list
- Gain an evangelist (Say what? Don't worry, I'll explain.)

But first, there are some myths I need to debunk.

Networking Myths

(Or: Never Ever Believe These Things)

Before we get to the nuts and bolts of *The 20-Minute Networking Meeting*, let's debunk some myths about networking and deconstruct some common mistakes. Here are some ways of thinking that you want to leave behind:

- Maybe I'm just wasting my time.
- Networking is just schmoozing.
- The longer the meeting, the better.
- It's helpful for *others* to have the chance to meet with *me*.
- A networking meeting is when I give a detailed description of my background.
- Off the cuff is best; I'll figure out each meeting when I get there.
- My networking contacts will find me a job!

Now let's deconstruct them.

"Maybe I'm Just Wasting My Time."

Pssst—remember the previous section? The part about how eighty percent of jobs are found through networking? Believe me, it's no waste of time.

Meeting with people (both new and old contacts) is probably the most important thing you can do while in transition. Your networking meetings could surely lead to job connections, but the networking meetings might also lead to potential consulting gigs, speaking engagements, and other business opportunities (not to mention friendship—a great networking connection). Your meetings will even get you caught up on some happenings in your industry. And feedback? Absolutely. You'll likely get a good understanding of how everyone else views you and your process. But these are just a *few* benefits of networking. So get rid of this mentality. Networking is never a waste of time.

⬦⬦⬦

Never let yourself believe that one person can help
you more than another, and never skip a networking
meeting. You never know who will yield the vital piece
of information or new contact that changes your career
forever. Networking is never a waste of time!

⬦⬦⬦

"Networking Is Just Schmoozing."

Mark this with a pen. Lots of executives commit the sin of schmoozing. Shooting the breeze is enjoyable, but not if you're the person who has work piling up back at the office. Unless you're looking for a job as a schmoozer, save the irrelevant chitchat. If you don't, you'll come across more as a social-minded networker than as a professional tracking down an employment opportunity. Worse, if you have "the gift of gab," you might run the risk of coming across as "salesy." Believe me: I see this often. And also believe me when I say it's irritating. Instead, present yourself and speak like the competent executive you are.

◇◇

Skip the schmoozing and irrelevant chitchat. While a social lead-in to the conversation is fine, don't leave the impression that you're more social-minded than professional.

◇◇

— MYTH —

"The Longer The Meeting, The Better."

I always grin when I hear this one. And then I watch the clock. Why? Because the meeting is long, that's why. Too long.

A networking meeting is a chance to make a positive connection. An hour-long litany about your background is not positive, and you will be seen as someone who doesn't "get it." That's not good. You can't forget that the person you're meeting with has a packed schedule. Taking an excessive amount of his or her time appears inconsiderate. It also reveals that you don't know how to run a crisp meeting (which harks back to my observation that so many networking meetings are not well-planned or well-run, and are ineffective and lack mutuality and gratitude). That's a lot of counts against you.

A long meeting shows that you lack consideration for your contact's time, and reveals that you don't know how to run a crisp, mutually beneficial networking meeting.

— MYTH —

"It's Helpful for *Others* to Have a Chance to Meet with *Me*."

Please—never expect that others will you see you as someone they need to impress. I see this mistake often. Remember that you're waiting for your next opportunity, and that an attitude of entitlement or expectation will backfire on you in grand fashion. While you may have had pull and influence in the past, it is important to remember that at this moment what you have to give in return is less than what you stand to earn. Which is fine. It's part of job transition. But consideration is key here.

Remember that every person who agrees to a networking meeting is giving you a gift. A *gift*. Think about it this way. If your contact works fifty hours per week, your meeting just made it a fifty-one-hour week. That extra hour is because of your meeting! That translates to less family time, less time for friends, and less time for other pursuits. But if that's hard to fathom, then ask what an hour means to you.

Another way to look at it: If the person is a consultant charging $250 per hour, a one-hour networking meeting with you just cost the person $250 in billable hours (or at the very least, an hour of selling time). How often do you give a gift worth $250? How often do you get this type of gift from someone you hardly know (such as your networking contact)?

◇◇

The time someone gives you is a gift. What does an hour mean to you? Is it worth $250 in billable hours? How often do you give a $250 gift? Don't take someone's schedule for granted; asking for time is asking for a gift and should be treated and appreciated as such.

◇◇

— MYTH —

"A Networking Meeting Is When I Give a Detailed Description of My Background."

No, it's not. Not if it isn't asked for. And even if it is asked for, there are rules around how much to share (which we'll get to later in the book). Networking is about *give and take*. You're there to learn as much as you're there to network.

This is important. You see, your networking contacts are probably not recruiters. Therefore, they think about jobs in fairly general buckets. CFO. University president. VP of marketing. They need to know just enough about your background to connect you with an opportunity if they are reminded of something relevant. Anything more than that makes things confusing and less memorable. Why?

It's simply too difficult to keep track of so much—especially if the purpose of the meeting is general networking.

◇◇◇

Listening is learning. Don't be tempted to talk all about yourself. Networking is give and take and not a detailed description of your background.

◇◇◇

— MYTH —

"Off the Cuff Is Best; I'll Figure Out Each Meeting When I Get There."

What executive would go into any meeting unprepared? Especially a meeting that could ultimately lead you back into employment? Now, you may be a fantastic orator, but that doesn't change the fact that you came across as unprepared. Weren't you always able to tell when someone came to you unprepared?

To a recruiter, it is immediately apparent when an executive is unready for a networking meeting. A CEO in transition came in for such a meeting with me, plopped down in the chair, and took off talking—how talented her peers felt she was, how skilled she was at change management, how strategic her vision was for her industry. I sat across from her and wondered how any of it was relevant to me. Now, don't get me wrong—I appreciate flexibility as much as the next person, but at least start with something structured. A quick overview of what you'd like to discuss, for instance, and a moment of pause to get the other person's approval of such an agenda. That alone would be fabulous.

An unprepared agenda will have undesired consequences.
Always be prepared for your meetings.

— MYTH —

"My Networking Contacts Will Find Me a Job!"

Most of your contacts are fulfilling their own job responsibilities. More often than not, those responsibilities are not recruiting responsibilities. Accept the fact that virtually none of your networking meetings will immediately lead to a current opportunity, and remind yourself that this isn't the point to networking anyway. It's about *ultimate*, not immediate, gratification. You simply want to get the "lay of the land." Bringing yourself up to date on what's happening in your industry is a good goal, for example, as is finding out who's out there, and who might be looking for you.

Think of it this way: If a friend of a friend called you right now to request a networking meeting, would you know of an immediate job opening for the person? Would you be prepared to help a bank president? An academic dean of social sciences? An operations exec in the packaging industry? Not likely. But when you *do* hear of an opening, you'll probably remember the new friend who requested a 20-minute networking meeting with you, right? Of course you will. And that person will remember you, too.

On recruiters: The same applies when you connect with us. The likelihood that any given recruiter will have an open assignment that fits your background is very, very small. You see, our work is nearly always dictated by the needs of our clients. We often don't even know what kind of job we'll be working on next. So how could we plug you into something we don't even know exists yet?

◇◇◇

Your contacts are not recruiters or hiring managers. Never expect a single networking meeting to lead to a job. Patience is the name of the game.

◇◇◇

Now that we've debunked some of the myths that surround networking, we'll focus on the hurdle that keeps job seekers from taking that first step. Let's start with a Real-World Perspective.

Real-World Perspective

("So You Want Me to Go Out There and Grovel, Huh?")

I got a call from an executive who happened to know my cousin. This individual, a senior vice president of supply chain, has an extensive background and pretty impressive accreditation. His job search, however, was at a standstill.

"How's the networking going?" I asked.

"It's nearly impossible getting responses from online applications," he expressed in frustration.

I let him know that online postings were rarely effective for executives (for the reasons you now know) and reassured him that he had a right to feel this way. Then I asked my question again.

"How is the networking going?"

Happy to have another opportunity to vent, he expressed the difficulties of getting through to recruiters. I smiled at this—it is a common gripe—and took the opportunity to explain that by nature of the industry we aren't outplacement counselors, nor do we exist to find jobs for executives in transition. Rather, we are here for our clients, much like any other business. It just so happens that our commodity of trade is execs. But in spite of his new understanding of this, I had to ask again.

"And, how is the *networking* going?"

It was as though he already knew the truth. He sighed and bottom-lined his answer.

"So you want me to go out there and grovel, huh?"

If I could only tell you how often I have heard this. Not just the tone of voice, but the mentality. No, it is not easy to ask for help. But it's not groveling, either.

No one is going to put opportunity in your lap, and there are no shortcuts. But as an executive, you already know this, don't you?

Now let's take a closer look at why this executive felt so discouraged by the thought of getting out there and networking.

What Makes
Networking
So Difficult?

*(Or: Okay, Okay, I'll Do It.
But It's So Hard!)*

Yes, networking is hard work. But you're not alone. I find most executives are hesitant to network. And when the purpose is to find a new job, they're even more reluctant.

Let's talk about this.

Maybe you don't like the idea of networking because you feel like you're intruding. Maybe you feel like your request for time is an unwelcome detour in someone's day. Or maybe you just don't feel like people want to sit with a stranger.

Very understandable. Really. Because your feelings are probably right. (I told you I was going to give you the perspective from the other side of the desk!) And there's a reason—a reason that was addressed at the very beginning of this book: Too many networking meetings are too long and too unfocused.

Long meetings simply don't honor the busy schedule of the other person. We've touched on this; ultimately, it's those meetings that give networking a bad name. Well, if you sat through a few of those, wouldn't *you* want to avoid taking networking meetings?

To compound this fear of networking, I find that many people are intimidated by the concept of it, too. Executives tend to envision an hour-long meeting, during which they need to be:

1. socially adept;
2. professionally impeccable; and
3. capable of the above without the need of an agenda.

If that were the case, you'd have to be a corporate and social genius armed with wit and improv skills, right? Well, no wonder you would be hesitant to network. Good thing that's not what we're talking about here.

Making Excuses

So what *am* I talking about? I'm talking about making contact, conducting brief meetings, and following up. *That's it.* It's something that, really, you've already been doing for years. Of course, the circumstances of networking are a bit different, but you can't let that get in your way. Yes, it's tough not to feel embarrassed or ashamed about being in transition, but it should *never* be a reason to avoid networking. Over the years, I've witnessed executives busy themselves with all sorts of "job-seeking activities" to avoid networking, all because of the feeling of embarrassment. You know these kinds of excuses—like rewriting a résumé or checking emails, or even shopping for a new pair of dress shoes that are "a must" before getting an interview! I assure you—I've heard them all.

So, what do you *do* to get rid of these fears and embarrassments? Simply commit to the steps in this book and have faith and remind yourself that no matter how well or poorly a networking meeting goes, you're already doing *much* more for your job search than before.

Three Real Perspectives on Networking

The idea of networking hits all of us differently. The following examples highlight three executive networking perspectives. I chose composite examples based on what I hear all the time. Here's what a few executives had to say, followed by my reactions.

Andre

Andre was recently laid off as the vice president of US operations for an electronic-components manufacturer. Andre is seeking a similar leadership position in operations and finds it slow going. While he has strong people skills, Andre is technically inclined and feels that technology can be his primary tactic toward finding a new executive position. Andre held a lot of pride in his previous position and grieves that he is no longer part of the team. He attended an executive briefing at our search firm.

"I hate the idea of being unemployed. And worse, I hate the idea of telling anyone I'm unemployed. I don't like talking about it. I don't want sympathy. What I am hoping is that I can find my next job by surfing the Internet without any help from anybody."

You can't really conduct an effective job search in a vacuum. People hire people, and making personal and professional connections is going to be the core strategy you need to find your next perfect job. Don't spend your time on the web. Frequently, I see executives spending too much effort looking at online job postings. It's networking that tells you what you need to know about your specific job market, and it's direct contact that puts you in front of decision makers.

MY SUGGESTION:

Try to limit your time in online postings to only an hour or two per week. Use the rest of your availability to pick up the phone, send emails, or have lunch with those who can help you make your next connection.

Jill

Jill, a vice president of sales, was recently fired after a disagreement with her boss, the company's owner. She isn't at liberty to say exactly what happened, but her boss is known to be difficult to work with. Whatever the situation, Jill is actively seeking a new position in a tough market, and is getting discouraged. I met her at a women's networking event and she shared her situation.

"My outplacement counselor wants me to start networking with people I used to associate with through my industry sales leadership group. The truth is, I don't really know those people very well. It's not that I mind talking to people. After all, that's what I do for a living. But, to call people I barely know and ask for time in the middle of their workday is going to be tough. I know how many hours a week these people work. And they travel a lot. How many of them are going to want to take time to meet with me? That's the part that gives me some hesitation to start my networking.

WHAT I SAID:

You're right about several things. Yes, you'll be contacting people you don't know well, and no, not all of them will have time to meet with you. But that's part of the nature of networking. I'm afraid that you'll just have to forge ahead with the caveats you've expressed. Start with the people you know best. Perhaps there are clients who you have "gone the extra mile for" over the years. Maybe you've assisted or trained some of your peers, or you could ask staff members you've mentored. Begin networking with people you are comfortable with and who will likely be receptive to your call.

MY SUGGESTION:

The model of *The 20-Minute Networking Meeting* recommends that you include how you can help others versus how others can help you. This is a difference-maker, and will help you feel like you're a partner and not a burden to the people you contact.

When you're ready, spend extra time on Key Question 5, about giving back to the people you meet with. (This can be found in the Great Discussion chapter.) Don't lose that sense of gratitude! It goes a long way with someone who puts a busy schedule on hold to meet with you.

Pat

Pat's position as chief financial officer was recently eliminated. He worked at a large commercial real estate developer. Pat serves on a nonprofit board with one of my colleagues, and called for some advice.

"I am a hard worker and I have been dedicated to my employer. I have worked sixty hours a week for the past decade, and I never complained. I focused on getting the job done and didn't take time to make many professional connections. Now that I need to start networking, I don't have people to connect with. I am going to have to contact people who are networked to my colleagues. I'm not a talker, either, and I don't always have the gift of gab—I'm no stand-up comedian and no politician. How am I going to keep these conversations going? I don't want to make a fool of myself."

WHAT I SAID:

Great question. But first, don't worry about having a limited network. Many people find themselves starting from the beginning. Even if you're not a talker, you'll do fine with the model of The 20-Minute Networking Meeting. *It's designed to help you construct and carry a conversation.*

MY SUGGESTION:

Sometimes executives feel that, despite their accomplishments inside their organization, they have not taken the time to build a network outside their organization. If you are on a nonprofit or professional board or committee, that's a start. So is your neighborhood. So is your faith community or civic group. Former staff and colleagues are great contacts. You probably have a broader network than you realize if you just consider who you already know.

OVERALL

Try to remember that networking is not about being aggressive or glib. It's about developing relationships through brief, meaningful interactions over the course of time. Doing that now is as good as any other time.

Now for the Good Stuff

So far, we've learned what networking is and why it works, and we've talked about a number of myths that surround networking for job seekers. We've also seen some examples of executives struggling with the idea of incorporating networking into their job searches. I hope you'll take a moment to think about your own job search, and try to identify ways some of these misperceptions have affected your search so far. But come back soon, because we're about to take a crash course in conducting the best networking meetings possible.

Now's the time for a quick coffee break.

Let's do it!

PART TWO

The 20-Minute Networking Meeting

Objectives & Strategy

You made it! We'll keep this short and get right to the nitty-gritty details. (Pssst—if you haven't read the first part of this book, we suggest you don't cheat. Shortcuts an executive does not take. Besides, Part Two will make more sense with the context provided by Part One.)

YOUR OBJECTIVE IN JOB NETWORKING

Okay, so you're in job transition. Your top-level objective is to land a new, terrific job, right? Sure. But what if your new networking contacts don't know of open positions in the first place? Then these are your objectives in networking:

- Gather new information
- Add new contacts to your list
- Gain an evangelist

Now let's take a closer look at each of these objectives and how they will help you achieve your *20MNM* goals.

Gather New Information

WHAT IT MEANS: Listening. Questioning. Absorbing (and writing down) what is said to you.

THE REASON: Networking is a way to learn from contacts firsthand. It's also a chance to share what you know with your contacts to get reactions and redirection. It's quite an opportunity. You'll be giving as much as you're receiving!

WHY YOU WOULD DO IT: How can you network if you're not in the know? And how can you receive if you're not willing to give? You always want a modest goal for gathering information from any one networking meeting. Every person will have a few nuggets of value for you. Examples would be:

- Information that informs you on changes in your functional area.
- Information that helps deduce who might be looking for help
- Information that keeps you abreast of your chosen industry or industries

VERY IMPORTANT:
Don't expect more than a few nuggets from each contact!
Remember, this is a brief *meeting*, not a seminar.

Add New Contacts to Your List

WHAT IT MEANS: Getting additional names. These could be:

- Other people in your and your contact's industry or function
- People in your target companies or industries
- Anyone else who could help in your job search

THE REASON: Contacts—especially the way we're defining the term here—are people who know you, specifically people who are connected somehow to your line of work, industry, etc. The more people who know you, the more information there is about you in the marketplace. The more your name is circulating in that marketplace, the more likely you will be connected to a great new opportunity.

WHY YOU WOULD DO IT: Because without expanding your network of contacts, you're going to be left in the dark. This is extremely important. Do you recall our scenario where Passive Candidate ended up in the glow of his computer while Active Candidate inserted herself into the radar of the working world? You want to avoid being like Passive Candidate.

VERY IMPORTANT:

Don't forget—most execs usually land their next job not from their own original list of networking contacts, or even from the contacts gained from that original group, but through networking in the "third ring" of people (i.e., friends of friends of friends). It's only through active networking that you'll get to the third ring. And, having worked with thousands of executives in transition, I, along with countless other executive recruiters, can attest that this is true.

Most executives find their next opportunity through the "third ring" of contacts (i.e., friends of friends of friends)!

Many years ago, I was looking for a new job. I was referred to a business consultant, and we set up a networking meeting. Since it was a fairly "distant" connection, I was anticipating a cordial but not extensive session. Imagine my surprise when she pulled out a large three-ring binder full of tattered pages containing all of her business connections. She proceeded to go through the binder name by name, page by page, offering many of these names to me as potential networking contacts. She must have given me twenty-five or more names! Top executives! One that I remember was a prominent CEO in a field related to my work. He took my networking meeting on her referral and we had a fine discussion. That meeting gave me the confidence to network with other CEOs. Some of the contacts I made from the names on those tattered pages turned into professional colleagues who later became clients. To this day, over fifteen years later, I remember the unexpected assistance from an unexpected source.

The lesson: You never know!

Gain an Evangelist

WHAT IT MEANS: A job seeker needs an evangelist, which is someone willing to take positive action on your behalf. Like your own personal ambassador, this is a person who will have a major impact on your networking. Developing one is something you must try to do with each new networking meeting.

THE REASON: Once you've got one on your side, you're on your way to twice the pay-off, but half the work. Here's what an evangelist might do for you:

- Forward your résumé
- Recommend you to someone who is hiring
- Check his or her company's internal postings to see if anything is a fit for you
- Contact you later with additional ideas
- Introduce you to someone else
- Suggest you for a project

WHY YOU WOULD DO IT: Why *wouldn't* you do it? Having someone who sings your praises, recommends you to personal contacts, and thinks of you first in a job search? Hmm. Not a lot to expand on here.

Now, despite what you may think, developing this kind of contact is very, very simple. People like to help people. For most of us, it's in our nature (though the desire wanes if our time is wasted). And most people in a position to help you likely got there because someone helped them first. So really, in a sense, they're not just giving, but giving back.

HOW YOU WOULD DO IT: Think about meeting new professional contacts. As you meet with those people, you will be there to learn and observe two things:

1. Their skills and abilities as related to what they do for a living;

2. How they act in a professional setting (we'll expand on that more in a second).

Now let's turn the focus to you. You'll be giving the same clear impression of how *you* act in a professional setting and you'll also leave an impression of what you have accomplished in the working world.

When these things line up and that new contact becomes convinced by your background and experience (not by selling or persuading) that you fit within their network somewhere, that person may become an evangelist.

Make sense? Let's put it in simpler terms, just for clarity's sake: When people really like you and have an appreciation for your work history and experience, they will likely go to bat for you. Especially if they sincerely believe your talent and offering should have a place somewhere in the working universe. Why would they do that? Because in the long run, having you in their network benefits them, too. When you're eventually in a position to give back in the way of business, it's a relationship that already has a foundation of trust and faith.

It is critical to keep in mind, however, that most of the time the people you are networking with are not interviewing you for a job. They will not be in a position to evaluate your skill set (they're not recruiters), nor will they evaluate your abilities and background against a particular hiring situation (because they're not interviewing you).

On the other hand, it is important that you don't treat a networking meeting as just a social interaction or a chance to make a new friend. Those things are fine, but your main objective in networking is to make a solid, positive impression about how you act in a professional setting.

Assuming that you are meeting a networking contact for the

first time, or reconnecting with someone you don't know well, you want to leave an impression that will prompt that person to recommend or refer you to others. Think about the executives you most admire. What are the characteristics that you admire about them? Think about your own positive professional characteristics. Do a few come to mind? Well, now is the time to show them. Here's what you want to come across in each networking meeting:

- You are positive (*upbeat tone, language, overall positivity*)
- You are strategic (*you know why you are there*)
- You are well organized (*by managing your meeting well, keeping a close tab on topics and time*)
- You are gracious (*appreciative and grateful for the time that was spent with you*)
- You follow through after a meeting (*prompt follow-up, meaningful ongoing interactions*)

Does this sound like someone you would recommend for a job or refer to a colleague? It does to me! You've heard the phrase "It's not what you know, it's who you know!" While that is certainly true in networking, there is a related sentiment that is equally true. "It's not what you say, but the impression you leave!" Leave 'em impressed!

Who You Are
(Or: Who You're *Supposed* to Be)

We've discussed your contacts and even touched on the angelic offerings of a potential evangelist. Before we get too far, however, have you given thought as to what type of executive *you* are? Are you someone who is well organized? Sharp? Do you manage projects and schedules effectively? Do you set and achieve objectives? Do others like being around you? Are you gracious to others? How about follow-up? Do you redirect and follow up again if need be?

The demands are certainly a tall order to fill, but if you've enjoyed the achievements of an executive career, you probably display all these characteristics and more. And now is the time to exhibit them. Why? Because in a networking meeting, you want to showcase your executive style as much as—if not more than—you want to carefully explain your skills and abilities. It's a big part of that overall impression. After all, would you hire someone with great skills and poor interpersonal style? No, probably not. So would you expect your networking contacts to endorse *you* if you displayed poor executive-style characteristics? No, probably not.

◇◇

CHARACTERISTICS YOU WANT TO EXHIBIT DURING YOUR NETWORKING MEETINGS:

Positivity
Strategic abilities
Impressive planning and organization skills
Strong communication skills
Generosity and gratitude
Follow-through

◇◇

Since we're on the topic of professional integrity, here's a great example of reputation and the power of evangelism. I call it:

"Everybody Loves This Guy!"

A few years back, I conducted an executive search for a company seeking a vice president of marketing in the consumer packaged-goods industry. I made over 150 calls to potential candidates and sources. The first person I called recommended a friend in transition who might be a fit. His name was Mark Stone. I already had Mark Stone in my database as someone to call, but I noted the recommendation anyway. It's important to keep track of these things.

Imagine my surprise when the tenth person I called also suggested Mark Stone. Then person number thirty-one. Then person number fifty-five.

In the end, eight people suggested that I call Mark Stone about this job. Eight.

Eventually, Mark Stone and I talked about the opportunity I was recruiting for. We discussed his background, interests, and credentials. Ultimately, the search I was conducting was not a fit, but with such an army of evangelists behind him, it's hard to avoid thinking of Mark when other marketing opportunities come up. While some time has passed, his name is *still* mentioned every time a related job opens up, whether he's a fit or not, due to his executive integrity and especially due to his legions of evangelists. They're doing work for him, and quite often, Mark doesn't even know it. I'm happy to report that Mark recently landed in a great new position. My guess is that he'll never be without a marketing opportunity in his career again.

The 20-Minute Networking Meeting

What It Is and Where It Came From

Since the publication of the Executive Edition a few years back, it has come to our attention that the *20MNM* generates controversy because it calls for so little time. The question most asked is: "Can one *really* cover that much ground in 20 minutes?" The answer is a resounding Yes, and we'll show you exactly how. But for the moment, allow me to explain how the material was culled from the experiences of others and actuated by a presentation I attended.

Invited to a business event that featured a local speaker and a topic I was interested in, I showed up prepared to pass the time. (Perhaps you do the same thing: Take articles to read, documents that need prep, and a cell phone full of emails to check). I assumed (just as everyone else did) that this was going to be a long talk, and I'd have time to catch up on other work. But I was in for a real surprise.

Just as the speaker seemed to get rolling, he finished. I remember thinking that I may have gotten there in the middle of his presentation. But everyone else seemed as surprised as I was (by the way we were all looking at one another), and the group eventually got out of their seats. We were actually *done!*

And that's when it hit me. The speaker's brevity wasn't just a welcome change to his presentation-going audience, but actually a slick strategy that brought sharp focus to his topic and made *effective use* of everyone's time. It was almost laughable in its effect! *People stuck around.* With extra time and the author's book on their hands, they were now free to be a self-engaged audience to come or go as they pleased, and many began asking meaningful questions about his material! And why wouldn't they? That was the whole reason they were there in the first place!

In retrospect, the speaker's outcome was even better than what I observed at the time. His book received a lot of exposure (I even passed it on to my colleagues), and better yet, I'm now relating the story of his book and presentation to *you.*

Now *that's* impact.

After leaving the event, I took some time to understand exactly what the speaker did to pull off such a feat. Here's what happened in all its simplistic glory. Somewhere after introducing his book (which he gave to all the attendees), the author threw out some juicy bits about its contents, pulled us in *juuust* enough to capture our interest, and then cut us free. From there, with no pressure to stay or involve themselves, the audience actually engaged, and *that was that.* It couldn't have been more perfect. Or short!

So often we attend professional presentations just *knowing* they're going to be too long, too detailed, or too irrelevant. Sometimes we want to go, and sometimes we have to.

Well, networking meetings can be the same in many ways. Occasionally people *want* to do them, and sometimes they feel that they *have* to. Many times, like a presentation, the meeting becomes too long, and if it's ill-planned or lacking in focus, it holds the *contact* captive, a waste of his or her time.

I contemplated this while considering the hundreds of networking meetings I had banked in the last few years, and asked myself, "Well, what *is* too long? What's too short? And is there a happy medium?"

As I slowly pulled this information together, I also *really* began to pay attention to the clock during meetings. I observed, more often than not, that people were pushing hour-long networking meetings—whether they had requested that much time or not. And once I came to *that* realization, I decided there had to be a better way.

My conclusion, as you know by this point, was that an hour is *a lot* for what actually needs to be discussed in a networking meeting. And as I began observing what an hour of networking time was taking away from me (work, which backed up; family time, which you can never get back once it's gone; social time with friends; and, for goodness' sake, *sleep*), I realized that it was all adding up to a lot of *life*. Heck, there are barely enough hours in the day for *work*!

So next, I began to distill. I gathered the best approaches that the best networkers brought to the table, and kept close track of the weakest methodologies. And of course, I did this while keeping track of time. This is what I found:

A full hour (even for an executive recruiter who is accustomed to this) *lost my attention*. Right around the thirty-minute mark, I started to consider what else I had to accomplish that day. Distraction quickly set in as I began to stress about the work piling up behind me.

Thirty minutes was better than an hour and, yes, I was less distracted, but it's still the length of a full TV sitcom (with commercials). And the mutual benefit was still too small. Where was the vital information about the networker? And why hadn't we hit those points in thirty full minutes?

Fifteen minutes was much better. Remembering the aforementioned speaker's short presentation, I focused on what my shorter meetings looked like. These weren't traditional networking meetings, but rather networkers dropping by or asking to just stop in and shake hands in the lobby. Fifteen minutes wasn't enough to learn about the people I was speaking with, and some of those precious minutes were being taken up by required hellos and proper goodbyes. And then I found the "happy medium."

Twenty minutes, as it turns out, is exactly the right amount of time to warm into a conversation, get a good sense of someone's background and goals, and see the person off properly. Over the course of time, this seemed to prove itself true, time and time again.

Not wanting it to be just my opinion, I shared the idea with my business partners and a few other heavy networkers. Universally, they concluded that this observation was spot-on. When the meetings were shorter they were better! Bingo!

After bringing the finer points of networking together (mind you, this is years' worth of networking) and collecting the experiences of a number of colleagues, a perfect, twenty-minute package of give-and-take networking emerged. Ultimately, it structured itself into *The 20-Minute Networking Meeting*. Which brings us to the book you're holding now.

The 20-Minute Networking Meeting is the distillation of decades of concepts. With the express goal of making each networking meeting do the most it can for you, it is specifically built for your job search, and designed to meet the needs of both networkers and their networking contacts. Follow this faithfully and you won't be let down. But don't get ahead of yourself. Stick to the model until you know it well.

Here are the golden rules. Remember:

- Each part is **important** and has a **purpose**
- There are **five steps** and **five questions**
- You should **follow them** *exactly* so that you get a command of the process

NOTE: As you become familiar with the *20MNM* format, you can allow yourself flexibility by tweaking your timing and agenda. Networking is a people activity. Conversations take turns and jump off topic. This is okay, so long as you use professional discretion to get back on track when you're too far off agenda. You won't always have to stick to 20 minutes. Until then, follow the steps!

What To Do First

Before you hit the job market and start the networking, you've got to be ready. Really ready. Do not begin networking (and certainly do not begin interviewing for jobs) until you're prepared.

How?

There are a lot of ways to be prepared to hit the job market—having an updated résumé and a prepared "elevator speech," planning your networking activities, identifying target organizations, among others. But the most important readiness factor before beginning the job search is your psychological state.

Psychological state? Yes, your psychological state.

This might be a delicate topic for some, but I have found that the vast majority of challenges to executive job seekers are issues relating to their psychological state. For nearly every job-seeker, being in transition is painful. Which is okay. After all, we're used to a particular rhythm of life that includes work, meetings, conferences, business travel, and deadlines (not to mention pride and identity). When it comes to an abrupt halt, it's understandably upsetting.

But this takes a toll and can sabotage your networking and job search efforts. A sad or depressed state is not a ready state. Again, the emotional roller coaster is natural; taking time to deal with it is acceptable, if not crucial. If you find that you still feel angry, down, or bitter, or you have no feelings about the situation at all, it's a bit too soon to begin networking. You could, of course, jump into things anyway, but mark my words when I say that it will have adverse effects on your meetings. Readiness is key.

Recently, I spoke with Pete, a chief information officer in transition. Pete reflected back on the early weeks of his unemployment and noticed in retrospect that he had felt and acted angry in some early networking situations. Though he may have had every right to feel angry about his situation, he made the mistake of taking that attitude into his meetings. What he found was that this affected *future* meetings. While his contacts and prior job post got him in the door initially, he noticed that the networking seemed to stop there. People just weren't willing to risk their own reputation by sending an unready person to other valuable people in their networks.

"I won't have a chance to go back and remake those first impressions," he told me. Unfortunately, he's probably right. Why make that same mistake if you can see it coming?

A while ago, I met with Jane, a candidate in job transition. Jane's manner of speaking was curt, her voice extra loud, and her gestures unusually expansive. She spoke at length about the faults of her prior employer. When I asked if perhaps she was struggling a bit with the change in her employment status, she slammed her hand on the desk. I literally jumped. Her voice was angry and the volume was high. "NO!" she yelled. She was actually shaking. I moved on to another topic, but concluded that any referrals to other networking contacts would be embarrassing for me and fruitless for her.

Now contrast Jane with Elaine, also an executive candidate in job search. Elaine was comfortable with her transition. While giving me her background, she explained her circumstances in a positive but matter-of-fact tone. There was no negativity or criticism of her former employer (trust me, I can make my own judgments and draw my own conclusions about such situations), and there was humor and laughter in our meeting. I actually had fun! Elaine was someone I definitely wanted to connect with my professional colleagues, and I knew that they would like her, too. Coming from a recruiter, someone whose network is her business, that's an important distinction when compared with an experience such as my meeting with Jane.

Bottom line: Take some time. Take control of your own transition and be strategic about your readiness. I don't need to tell you that it's impossible to be a confident leader when you're lacking confidence in yourself. Be ready.

For practice, go to the Readiness Exercise on page 145 to help you assess your own readiness to step back into the job market. Once you've spent some time with these questions and feel confident in your answers, come back as we dive into the framework of *The 20-Minute Networking Meeting*.

Real-World Perspective Like He Read My Mind — a 20-Minute Meeting

Eureka!
I was beginning to think that there wasn't a single executive in my city who knew how to network effectively. That is, until recently when I met with Bert.

Bert and I work in related industries. We know several people in common, though I'd only met him one other time before he asked to meet and discuss a change at his organization and his future career plans. Right off the bat, Bert made a positive impression and a reasonable request. I was happy to say yes to the meeting.

Bert arrived a few minutes early and was chatting with our office manager when I came into the lobby. We exchanged greetings and settled into the conference room.

Before we even got started, Bert thanked me for my willingness to meet with him. He reminded me that his purpose was to let me know about some changes in his organization and to relate some of his current thoughts about his own career direction. He shared with me that his organization's parent company was intending to close the local office. He and his co-president felt strongly about keeping the office in the local community, so Bert had decided to support his co-president as the leader of the new organization and to participate only as a silent partner.

Moving on to explain how this could affect him down the road, Bert briefly shared his thoughts about his next career move. He had a couple of specific questions for me, things that he hoped I could clear up or explain about his career choices. I'm a visual person, so I grabbed a pen and sketched out my thoughts while I talked. It's a different approach, but he appreciated it.

"Seeing it laid out like that clarifies a lot," he said. He then thanked me for my input. In return, Bert shared a few ideas that were helpful to me in my business, letting me know which companies in the area were looking to hire new executives.

Then, before I knew it, Bert was thanking me again.

"I don't want to take too much of your time," he said, closing his folio. "I really just wanted to update you on my situation and get your input on those couple of questions." He stood up from his seat, but continued. "I will update you in a couple of weeks. In the meantime, I'll forward the name of that potential client. Thanks again, very much."

I stood with him and we shook hands. All done. The meeting was fun, thorough, efficient, and helpful to us both. And wouldn't you know it—a glance at my watch showed it had lasted twenty minutes!"

Your 20-Minute Networking Meeting Cheat Sheet

All **right, now we're rollin'.** Here's a very brief overview of what's coming. This cheat sheet will be available again at the end of the book for easy reference. (See page 144.)

Note the time frames for each step. *The 20-Minute Networking Meeting* is really this simple. It consists of five parts:

STEP 1:	**Great First Impression**	2–3 minutes
STEP 2:	**Great Overview**	1 minute
STEP 3:	**Great Discussion**	12–15 minutes
STEP 4:	**Great Ending**	2 minutes
STEP 5:	**Great Follow-Up**	After the Meeting

And that's it!

Each one of these steps will be detailed in the pages to come, letting you know what to do, how to do it, and why.

FIRST UP: STEP 1— Great First Impression

Step 1—
Great First Impression

GOAL:	To make a great first impression
HOW:	With thanks and short chitchat
TIME LIMIT:	2 to 3 minutes
WHAT YOU WILL DO:	Arrive, express gratitude, highlight connections, set the agenda
NOTE:	Turn to page 149 for your Great First Impression Planner

ARRIVING FOR YOUR 20-MINUTE NETWORKING MEETING

Arrive a few minutes early. If you're meeting at a coffee shop or restaurant, arrive as early as you'd like. If you're meeting at your contact's office (I'm speaking from experience here), don't arrive *too* early.

THE REASON: If you're meeting at a public place, you can do as you please. But if you're meeting at your contact's office, it can be uncomfortable for your contact to know that someone is waiting in the lobby—especially if he or she has work to do before the meeting. At my firm, we've had people arrive up to forty-five minutes early.

It's not our habit to keep our guests waiting, but giving up lunches or a much needed break to start a meeting way ahead of the scheduled time isn't exactly something we care to do, either. It can result in a networking meeting with an annoyed and distracted contact.

WHAT TO DO: If you find yourself with extra time, find a place to sit and work outside the office. Review your notes for your meeting. Take a stroll around the block to collect your thoughts. Maybe you'll even see something interesting to talk about in your meeting.

Here are some other things to concern yourself with until your appointment:

- Double check: Do you have your résumé, pen, and notebook?
- Are you prepared for the questions and topics that you wish to discuss?
- If you're in the office, take a look around. What do your surroundings tell you about this organization and its culture?

◇◇

TIP:
Familiarizing yourself with your environment will help
you feel more comfortable before your networking
meeting begins. Take a look around!

◇◇

Don't be fooled. Your first impression starts the moment
you arrive for your meeting. Be respectful toward
anybody who greets you (assistants, front desk people).
This is essential to remember because often
your contact will ask their opinion of you.
("Was she friendly? Courteous? Appreciative?")

EXPRESSING GRATITUDE

Before there is any networking discussion, share a hearty smile
and a firm handshake during your introduction. And look your
contact in the eye. You'd be surprised how often I get feedback
from clients telling me that executive candidates have inadequate
eye contact.

Once you get a lock on that, express your gratitude. Perhaps
you already thanked your contact by email or over the phone when
you set up the meeting, but it's always best to offer thanks again.

THE REASON: Remember—this person is giving you the gift
of time. Acknowledging that fact in a sincere manner will earn
you a lot of respect and gratitude in return. As far as how to
express your thanks, you can do that any way you'd like. But here
are a few examples to start with.

"It is great to see you, Ed. Thank you again for meeting with me."

"Nice to meet you, Christine. I so appreciate your time today."

*"Hi, Joan! What a great office! Again, thank you for agreeing to
see me."*

All right, so now you have a grip on introductions. Next . . .

HIGHLIGHT CONNECTIONS

Though your meeting may start with a little small talk around the artwork in the lobby or the scenery you saw outside, a better way toward a great impression is by highlighting mutual connections.

THE REASON: If you don't know the person you are meeting with all that well, it can be a safe way to bridge the gap. People feel more comfortable knowing that they have acquaintances in common. And there are many ways to make this connection, so don't worry if you don't have a close connection to your contact.

WHAT TO DO:
- Remind the other person of who connected you in the first place:

  "Joaquin Thomas asked to send his greetings. Joaquin has been a great mentor to me and he said you were a great mentor to him."
- Mention other people you know in common:

  "I think we might have some folks in common at Zortiss Marketing. Do you know Kyle Daniels and Francie Walters?"

If you find yourself in a position in which you have no one in common, you can try these approaches:

- Suggest other likely professional connections:

  "I think you and I may have some common professional colleagues, since we've both been active in the local chamber of commerce."

- Ask about a person you both may know (but only if you think it is likely; don't do this just for sake of banter):

  "I understand you used to be at ABX Carpet. Do you happen to know Harry Henderson?"

Or, if appropriate, you could make a personal connection. (By appropriate, I mean that crossing personal boundaries could come across as creepy and make your contact uncomfortable.)

"Your website bio mentioned that you live in River's Edge. I've lived nearby in Riverside for about ten years."

Or:

"I read that you're an alum of Stateside University. Our daughter began school there just a few months ago."

TO REPEAT: You should use the last example only if you believe it would be well received. Taking your professional networking meeting into the personal realm can be a powerful tool, but it can backfire easily if your contact does not care to discuss anything other than business.

At this point, you now have your introductions behind you. What's next? Get to the point. (And feel free to state you're doing so!)

SETTING THE AGENDA

Here it is—the moment of (literal) truth. Tell your contact you're only going to take twenty minutes, and say exactly what you're hoping to talk about in that time.

THE REASON: As you've already read in this book, most executives expect a networking meeting to take an hour. Even when someone says, "Really, just a few minutes of your time." However, you can reaffirm your promise by laying out an actual agenda ahead of time. This will help your contact believe that you'll keep to your promise of twenty minutes.

Here are a few more reasons why setting the agenda is important.

It will set the tone of:
- The meeting
- The impression you create
- Your overall job-search approach

In addition, it will show that you are:
- Prepared
- Considerate of your contact's time
- Unafraid to lead

WHAT TO DO: Introductions and gratitude out of the way, hit the seats and start the meeting. Again, convey that you only need twenty minutes.

REMEMBER: The person is doing you the courtesy of meeting with you. Return the courtesy by acknowledging that fact.

Let's see what a couple of examples would look like (and don't worry—you don't have to get too fancy with it):

"Good morning, Jack. I just need twenty minutes of your time. I want to give you a brief overview of my background and ask a few questions that help in my job search."

"This will be brief, Laura. I just hope to mention a few of my career highlights and get your perspective on a few things that relate to my job transition."

And that's it. Really! If you care to be a little more specific, you can do so. But keep it short and crisp, and stick with the two-minute timeline you have for this step.

REAL-WORLD PERSPECTIVE

Networking executive Delmar used the principles of *The 20- Minute Networking Meeting.*

"The most valuable part for me was having an agenda with a focus on a series of steps," he said.

The fixed amount of time for each step kept him from going off on tangents and kept the meeting active and on point.

"If I started to slip on time," he explained, "I got back on track, knowing what part of my agenda was next."

Delmar compares the structure for a networking meeting to orchestrating a presentation.

"You need a structure to do it well."

A VERY IMPORTANT SIDE NOTE:

Though it is important to make your agenda clear, please remember that you *do* have flexibility if you need it. I know I've expressed this notion before, but if your introduction goes well, and your chitchat extends past your first two minutes, that's *totally okay!*

But be sensitive—if your chatting goes for five minutes or more, do your best to get things back on track and not overstay your welcome. The only exception here is if your contact is leading your talk.

◇◇

◇◇

IMPORTANT:

Don't wait for your contact to start the discussion! You called the meeting and it is your responsibility to manage it. After all, would you agree to attend a meeting called by someone else and then be expected to run it yourself? Probably not. Be the leader that you want to be and lead!

◇◇

MARCIA'S PERSPECTIVE — WHERE IS THE AGENDA?

An executive in transition came in for a meeting and plopped down in the chair across from me. We exchanged a few pleasantries, and then . . . nothing. No agenda, no plan for the meeting. At the time, I was writing this very book on effective networking. Because it was not my responsibility to lead this person's meeting,

I let the awkward silence play out, wondering if this executive, previously in a CEO position, would catch on and grab hold of the meeting. He did not. A number of explanations strolled through my mind, but it struck me as strange that a CEO would ask for a meeting and expect me (or some other person) to run it. It did not leave me with a good impression.

In the end, I found a way to participate in the meeting anyway, and even gave the person a helpful suggestion or two. But I did not offer any networking names. My thought was that if I sent him to any of my contacts, he would conduct himself the same way. My contacts are too important to me, and I could not have them thinking I endorse such behavior. Bound by that fear, I was forced to play it safe, and meted out only minimal assistance. I know by experience that this job seeker left our meeting with some sense of "success," having networked and gained a couple of tips. But he lost the chance to get some meaningful contacts, and certainly to gain an evangelist.

Why didn't I help him more? Why didn't I take the time to teach him how to conduct a networking meeting?

The answer is simple: It's not a professional service for offer. There are, in fact, outplacement consultants and career coaches who work with executives to help them plan and execute their job search.

The people you are networking with are not likely to be professional career coaches and résumé writers. That is not their job. It is *your* job to have the right resources to help you frame up your job search and to conduct the meetings you request.

NEXT UP: STEP 2 — Great Overview

Step 2 —
Great Overview

GOAL:	Give a great overview of your background
HOW:	Providing a crisp, brief, and memorable understanding of your work experience
TIME LIMIT:	1 minute (Yes, one minute. No more!)
WHAT YOU WILL DO:	Briefly state your experience
NOTE:	Turn to page 152 for your One-Minute Overview Planner

BREAKING DOWN YOUR ONE MINUTE

Right about here you're probably still reeling over "one minute." "Whoa, whoa," you may say. "But I've got thirty years of experience!"

Yup. Totally get it. And that experience is valuable. However, it is not valuable to give a lengthy oration with detailed discussion of your experiences during a 20-minute networking meeting.

THE REASON: Because a one-minute overview is efficient and strategic. The objective of the one-minute overview is to give the other person a general sense of what you've done. With a clear-as-day, clean-as-a-whistle, one-minute overview, your contacts will think about where you "fit" jobwise when they hear of an opening. It also helps them think about others you might want to connect with, without bogging them down with additional details that may be irrelevant for this kind of meeting. You're networking, not interviewing. In addition, it keeps things to a minimum so that you may discuss the real information you're after.

REMEMBER: The objective of the networking meeting is to gather information, gain a contact or two, and (hopefully) create an evangelist. It is not to share your entire work history. Stick with one minute!

"Gosh," you say. "Is one minute really possible?"

Yes! Here's how.

WHAT TO DO:
- Tally your years in your particular job function
- Highlight your background
- Follow with where (organizations) you've worked
- Tie those with the most recent titles you've held
- String them all together

Here they are again, with examples.

- **Think number of years in the function:**
  "Overall, I've got twenty-three years in the technical sales function."

  "I was in operations management for ten years before moving into general management for the last twelve years."

- Consider the highlights of your background:

    "I made President's Club for sales excellence ten years in a row at Xerox."

    "I was proud to be the founding CEO at a plastics company in Milwaukee. We brought 100 new jobs to an ailing part of town."

- Followed by places you've worked:

    "I've been at large companies like Xerox as well as smaller distributors."

    "I have worked at some of the most respected parts manufacturers in our region."

- Tied in with most recent titles you've held:

    "I've been VP of sales most recently."

    "My most recent title was CEO; before that, I was general manager."

Getting a feel for it? Here are three more examples of the high-level view of information you want to share regarding your specific experiences, skills and abilities.

"I'm a twenty-year training professional specializing in leadership development."

"I am a senior financial executive with background in international manufacturing companies."

"My fifteen-year experience is as an operations leader in electronics with general management background and a Six Sigma black belt."

HERE'S A TIP: Your one-minute overview could also include references to any people or places that you have in common with the networking contact:

"ExCo is where I worked with our mutual friend Joe Jones."

"I saw that you were at IBM in the 1980s. I was there at the same time, from about '84 to '88."

"I got my CPE certification in 2001, working with Jeanne McGuff. It's through her that I was connected to you."

◇◇◇

There's always flexibility in how you present yourself.
All examples are only meant to be a guideline.
If you like them, use them! If you want to put
your own flair on it, do so!

◇◇◇

REAL-WORLD PERSPECTIVE

Dave is a fellow recruiter and frequent networker. He reiterated the importance of a brief overview.

"I don't want to hear the full story of their background," he told me when I interviewed him for this book. And it's not because Dave isn't interested in hearing the person's experience.

"It's just that I don't have the time."

Dave is a really nice guy who cares about people. I know this because I know him.

"I would like to hear more," he went on, regretfully. "But I can't. These days, even the *Reader's Digest* condensed version is a little too long."

Another executive who is frequently asked to network with others shared the same sentiment but has a very different reaction to a long-winded overview.

"It's a red flag," Sharon said of a personal story that gets too long. An executive director of a fast-growing professional services firm, she sees time management and self-management as a number-one priority. "And if they are too into their story, something isn't right."

BOTTOM LINE: Shorten the overview. A lot.
Yes, a minute is a relatively short time, but by reading the above, it should be clear how quickly, efficiently, and accurately you can describe your work history. Just practice. Rehearse. Time yourself. You will be surprised at what you can convey in just sixty seconds.

SAMPLES OF ONE-MINUTE OVERVIEWS

A suggestion: Read them out loud and time them.

EXAMPLE 1— KARLA

"Nice to meet you, Charise. I believe I already sent you my résumé. There's a lot more detail there, but basically, I'm a nonprofit CEO with twenty years of experience in the sector. I'm currently heading up the organization called Serve the Youth, where I've been for the last ten years, CEO for the last five. We have a budget of $45 million and operate out of three Midwest cities. With a staff of around fifty people in each city, we provide job training for at-risk youth as well as 'get started' assistance with financial planning and life skills. Prior to joining Serve the Youth, I was the director of high school remedial programs in the Lodge Lake School System. Ideally, I'd like to stay in the nonprofit sector. My passions are for education, youth, and community development."

How did that sound? Speaking that overview out loud takes around forty-five seconds!

EXAMPLE 2— SCOTT

"Thank you again for taking the time to meet with me. I've been in consumer marketing since I got my MBA from Michigan State University in 1990. After five years at General Mills in product marketing, I went to a smaller foods manufacturer and focused on foods marketing to nontraditional channels, such as drug and discount stores, clubs, and dollar stores. I loved the nontraditional retail environment and I've stayed there ever since. The last three years, I've been VP of sales and marketing with See-Go Brands, leading a national team selling into retail and helping introduce new products in the organic foods arena. I'm ideally looking for a sales or marketing leadership role that is consumer product based."

How about that one? Time to spare!

REMINDER: For an exercise in how to put together a one-minute overview, turn to page 152. It will walk you through the process.

NEXT UP: STEP 3 — Great Discussion

Step 3 — Great Discussion

GOAL:	Have a short but great discussion
TIME LIMIT:	12–15 minutes
WHAT YOU WILL DO:	Talk through Five Key Questions. You will draft Key Questions 1–3 yourself, using *The 20-Minute Networking Meeting* structure. Then, I will tell you exactly what to ask in Question 4 and Question 5. *(We'll get to specifics in a second. Here's some prep first.)*
NOTE:	Turn to page 158 for your Great Discussion Planner

GREAT DISCUSSION

As you can deduce, most of *The 20-Minute Networking Meeting* is spent in discussion. Still, you shouldn't spend any more than fifteen minutes in this part of the meeting. Admittedly, a robust discussion can—and typically does—last more than twelve to fifteen minutes, but to respect the other person's schedule, and to keep to your promise, be flexible, but stay on target. The only exception is if your contact is leading the discussion and it seems rude or counterproductive to get things back on track. In that case, just let things flow. But pay attention for signs indicating your contact is ready to wrap up the meeting!

WHAT YOU SHOULD KNOW

THIS IS IMPORTANT: During your meeting, never, under any circumstances, ask for information that you should already know. We alluded to this earlier in the book, but it bears repeating. This includes general info about your contact's company, the economy, political climate, news reports, or anything that a newspaper or the Internet could readily tell you.

THE REASON: Your contact reads the papers, too, and, like you, probably is aware of the business happenings in your region and the general business climate overall. But how unfortunate (embarrassing) would it be if you were completely clueless about such information (especially concerning your contact's organization)? You are there hoping to make a good impression!

On the other hand, with a busy executive schedule, your contacts might have far less time to learn what's happening with specific organizations, new products, up-and-coming sectors, or possibly (believe it or not) the trends happening right in his or her own industry. A little extra effort researching these areas will go a long way.

Think about it—could this have been you at some point? Were you always familiar with the latest trends or the newest happenings in the market? Did you know the thought leaders and visionaries in your function? Probably not all the time. So why would it be any different for any other busy executive?

There is great material available that can form a foundation for your discussion—and that is the whole point of the fifteen-minute middle of your networking meeting.

WHAT TO DO: Homework. Research these categories *beforehand*—and never ask about them during the meeting:

- The overall economy and business climate
- The job market
- Political changes that affect your industry or job function
- Generally available information about your industry or job function
- Readily available information about the organization and the person you're meeting with

KNOW THE PERSON YOU'RE TALKING TO

It's extremely disappointing when someone comes to meet with me and doesn't really know who I am or what I do. Or, who hasn't even taken the time to view my bio on my company's website. As much as possible, you should know the person you're talking to.

THE REASON: It's rude if you're unfamiliar with the person you're asking assistance from. You somehow believed I could help you, yet you know nothing about me?

One of my professional friends, Barney, is about as well-connected as they come, and as a consultant he is often asked to meet for networking. He, too, notices how people use the time in a networking meeting.

"If someone asks to meet with me and starts by saying, 'So, what do you do?'" he says, "our meeting suddenly becomes awfully short!"

WHAT TO DO: More homework.

Here are a few things someone would learn about me from my bio on my company website:

- My job title and specialty areas
- How long I have been with my firm
- The other jobs I have had
- My educational background
- Nonprofit boards that I serve on
- Professional memberships and certifications I have

As you can see, that's a lot of fodder for great discussion, taken directly from my company bio. And that's just from the company website alone! If the individual also checked my LinkedIn page, he or she would have learned even more, including:

- The number of years I spent at each of my previous employers, along with my actual job titles
- Some of my professional interests
  (i.e., what LinkedIn groups I belong to)
- How networked I am (i.e., how many people I am linked with)
- People we know in common
- Professional books I've endorsed
- People I've recommended
- A lot more

Now, your contact might not have this level of information readily available, but in the age of social media, it's rare to find absolutely nothing about your contact someplace online. Take the time to get to know the person you're meeting with.

REAL-WORLD PERSPECTIVE

Quinn is a fellow business owner and frequent networking contact who shares my belief in the importance of good planning. When executives don't take the time to learn who she is and what she does before a networking meeting, it's a big disappointment.

"When I meet with people, I ask them whether they have visited my company's website." When the occasional executive admits that she or he hasn't, Quinn, none too shy with her feelings or thoughts, asks, "Why not?"

The message here is obvious, but if you don't like the idea of being put on the spot, be prepared. Even Quinn hopes that by asking such a potentially embarrassing question, the networker will not make the same mistake in future meetings.

KNOW THE COMPANY

It's safe to assume that when it comes to networking, a contact's company is just as important as the contact. That's to say, help from a contact in a different industry—or from a contact at a consulting company, or from someone who is unemployed—might come in a format different from that of a peer or colleague in the same industry. But if the company is a fast-growing Fortune 500, for example, it gives a lot of weight to who your contact is and what role he or she plays in the organization. So, again, knowing about the company is just as important as knowing about your contact, regardless of the organization's size.

THE REASON: Think about how unfortunate (embarrassing) it would be to arrive at your contact's office not knowing what the company does.

WHAT TO DO: Homework. Here are some examples of things you should know (just to name a few):

- Recent important events
- Press releases
- Key customers
- New product introductions
- Milestones
- Pending deals
- Positive news write-ups

HOW TO DO IT: The web is a miraculous source of information. Many company websites contain press releases that will detail recent events and even mention new customers or business relationships. They, of course, will also mention new products (if that isn't the first thing you see on the website).

KEEP IN MIND: The more you know, the better the impression you will leave. Now, that's not to say you need to have a night of memorization before your morning meeting, but knowing key points that are important to the organization (milestones, pending deals, positive news write-ups) can only help. Just think: How flattered would *you* be if someone came to your office knowing something meaningful about your organization and the things you've helped it accomplish? Wouldn't you be more willing to help this person? (And if you didn't think about it yet, you can also see how this can help create an evangelist!)

There are five questions that will provide the structure for the discussion part of your networking meeting. Before we get to them, however, we must touch on some questions that you should *never* ask. These are the questions that have become the boring standard in business and networking meetings. They're not necessarily deal-breakers, but they will define you as the same as any other executive who didn't "have the time" or put forth the effort to do some homework. Avoid these and you will stand out in good fashion.

Here they are. (Some of these repeat things we've already mentioned, but there's no hurt in re-reminding.)

- **Do not ask (general) questions about things you should already know.** This includes things about the economy, well-known trends in your industry, and so on. You could, however, ask for your contact's reaction to something you've read or heard on a given topic (choose carefully). It's always good to encourage thoughts and opinions of a contact.

- **Do not ask for work history or background overview.** Your contact is not being interviewed—don't make him or her feel that way, especially if you're the one looking for work. Find out the person's background yourself!

- **Do not ask what the contact's company does, or how business has been lately.** You should know this already. Otherwise, why would you think this person could help you?

- **Do not ask how the two of you are connected.** You should already know this. It's your responsibility to remind your contact about personal or professional connections.

- **Do not ask, "What do you think about my résumé?"** Besides putting someone on the spot, it's not really relevant. Why? You're not being interviewed. An appropriate person to ask for feedback on your résumé would be an outplacement counselor or a job coach.

- **Do not ask personal questions without a purpose.** "Do you have children?" is not a suggested icebreaker.

- **Do not ask the contact to divulge any information about the organization that should not be shared in a relatively new relationship,** such as specific plans for upcoming lay-offs, upcoming product launches, personnel changes, and the like.

REAL-WORLD PERSPECTIVE

Remember Barney, my well-connected consultant friend? Barney evaluates the level of preparation a person in transition has put into the meeting. He anticipates that the person has "pre-thought" the meeting and therefore is "able to comment on what they have learned about me, my company, my profession, and the like." The amount of preparation affects Barney's willingness to share leads and suggest other executives to call.

"None of my connections would ever hire someone unprepared for an interview," Barney explained. "A networking meeting, to me, is a clear indicator how someone would act in a future interview."

Even if your approach would be different, would you be willing to risk that impression?

FIVE KEY QUESTIONS 1 – 3

The first three questions in your discussion, called Questions 1, 2, and 3, are intended to guide the very important discussion portion of your networking meeting. A short, productive discussion can be difficult for many job seekers. This is often surprising, given that most executives do a great job managing meetings and asking questions when at work.

So how do you have a meaningful discussion that is still clean and crisp while you're networking? By formulating your first three questions from the prep you've done before the meeting.

These first three key questions are questions that you will write yourself, following *The 20-Minute Networking Meeting* structure. They will be designed based on the specific person you are meeting with. These questions will be completely up to you, but they must be unique for the contact you're meeting with.

Why? To gain the unique wisdom or specific knowledge that you wish to learn from this particular contact. These are never questions that address common knowledge, or something that could be found during your prep work. Instead, they are thought-out, courteously asked inquiries specific to your contact that, perhaps, only your contact could answer.

Where's a good starting point for such carefully designed questions? Your contact's bio or LinkedIn profile, or even the contact's company website. Read through them carefully, and the moment you wonder about something, jot it down. From here you can formulate dynamic, thought-provoking questions.

Here's such a scenario:

You're perusing your contact's LinkedIn profile and realize that she has certifications that you've considered getting. Formulating a question around this will not only give you something to talk about, but it will provide a solid piece of information that will help you in the future.

HOW TO STRUCTURE THESE QUESTIONS

These specific contact questions come in two parts. The first part is an **observation** (or a piece of information), and the second part is the **related question** (or a request for comments from the contact).

Here is an example for the above scenario.

- *"Sally, you have your SPHR certification* (**observation**). *Has that been valuable to you and would you suggest I pursue it at this stage of my career* (**related question**)?"*

Make sense? You've pointed out your observation and then you've asked a thought-provoking question related to it. Here are more examples:

- *"You have transitioned from a corporate CFO to a similar role in a nonprofit organization (**observation**). Assuming I am also interested in moving from corporate to nonprofit, do you have any pearls of wisdom for me (**related question**)?"*
- *"Hector, you've been in marketing communications roles in both health care and financial services organizations (**observation**). How do you compare the need for internal marketing communications professionals in those two sectors (**related question**)?"*
- *"I'd also like to ask your opinion about commercial real estate management. You came from a more traditional background into the field (**observation**). How do you think my background would be received if I were to explore opportunities at real estate management firms like EO Operations or Regional Management Services (**related question**)?"*

- *"We both hold a Six Sigma black belt (**observation**). I sort of feel that interest in the Six Sigma methodology is waning (**observation**). Do you feel that (**related question**)? How has your organization evolved in its use of Six Sigma (**related question**)?"*
- *"I noticed you spent four years in management consulting before accepting your current role as president (**observation**). How was it for you stepping into and out of consulting (**related question**)? Is that a path that you would recommend (**related question**)?"*

WHAT THE STRUCTURE DOES

Placing the *observation* (first part of the question) at the beginning of your questions establishes the fact or point you're addressing. This gives the listener the heads-up as to where you're going. The *related question* (second part of the question), in turn, evokes the person's assistance, thereby sparking discussion. In simpler terms: You give a heads-up about what you're going to ask, then you ask for the other person's thoughts.

Tip: Asking a second related question, as in the last two examples, is perfectly acceptable. However, it's important to remember that your meeting is not a question-answer session. Sometimes it's best (even strategic) to let your contact answer your first question before you follow up with your second question—if the person didn't already answer it in the process of answering the first. This way you won't put your contact on the spot or give the impression you have a list of questions to answer. It also helps bring more depth to your discussion by delving further into your topic.

TIP:

Sometimes, you can reuse your great discussion questions in multiple networking meetings. This might be valuable if, for example, you would like to get more than one perspective on a matter of great interest to you in your search. You must still think carefully about the questions you select for each networking meeting. Don't ask similar questions for lack of planning!

REAL-WORLD PERSPECTIVE

Sophie is the president of a consortium of companies in the steel manufacturing space.

"I do a fair bit of networking with executives in transition as part of my role as president of a large trade association. My association posts some positions on our website, and I am often privy to other openings on a somewhat confidential basis.

"While I don't mind taking these meetings, I am constantly surprised by how poorly prepared some of the networkers are. People show up and they are very happy about the meeting and pleasant to talk to, which seems to make the meeting go a little long. I don't have a problem with that, but I do have a problem when people arrive without a sense of who I am or what my company does. The lack of preparation renders them less able to manage the meeting effectively, and—here is my hot button—when someone requests a meeting with me and spends the time asking me about my own background, it can feel like I'm being interviewed! I wonder if these people do this in their real jobs—do they call meetings and show up unprepared and let the other person do the talking? I mean, how long would it take to do some basic planning ahead of time? Sometimes it's as though job seekers seem to lose their ability to plan along with losing their job. It's extremely frustrating."

FIVE KEY QUESTIONS: QUESTION 4

Your fourth question will help you with a major objective for the meeting: expanding your network. Essentially, you'll be asking your contact to recommend the names of some individuals whom you can reach out to. This question will be similar each time you ask it, but slightly tailored on a case-by-case basis. The gist is to ask for further networking contacts.

This is where networking breaks down for a lot of job-seeking executives. It's where I've seen a lot of people freak out. The general consensus is: *"It was hard enough asking for the meeting itself! If I ask for names of other people, I'm gonna look desperate."*

That's not true. That's how business works—give and take. Second of all, this feeling (and the excuses that come with it) isn't unusual, so there's nothing to worry about here. In fact, I've heard these same protests for as long as I can remember (along with *"No one wants to give names of other people,"* and *"This part is just too uncomfortable!"*). But you have to admit that not a day of business goes by when people aren't doing this very thing on every level in every industry out there. Looking at it from that standpoint, there's no reason to avoid asking the question.

Having said that, I want to acknowledge that getting started isn't all that easy. So, here are a couple of tips to deal with the fear.

- Remind yourself that the people you meet with have also had to find a job at one time too. Some more than

once. They know the value of networking. They get it.
- Remind yourself that these people said yes to a meeting with you in the first place. They likely know that you will be asking for names of contacts.
- Because they know the drill, they may even have come prepared with some names in mind.

REAL-WORLD PERSPECTIVE

Jerlyn is a business owner who often meets with executives in her industry. She told me that she expects a networking meeting to include a request for other contacts.

"I come prepared with some ideas," she told me. "But the 'ask' is important, too. I won't give the names without the question."

WHAT HAPPENS IF THEY SAY NO?

Well, then they say no (which is the worst that can happen). A gracious thank you will suffice, and then you simply move on to your next and final question.

Let's get to some examples. If the general question that you want to ask is "Who else do you know that might be a good contact for me in my job search?" you could probably go ahead and just say as much. But put a little more consideration behind it, and you might get a much better response.

Here are some ways to ask:

- *"Do you know of anyone from your work on the engineering conference who might be a good connection for me?"*
- *"Is there anyone here in the product development side who might be a useful person for me to call?"*
- *"You used to work for JPN. Are there any former colleagues there whom I should touch base with?"*

Notice the phrasing in those questions. They're direct, yet considerate. They're not blunt, but they're totally clear. Word choice is needed. Sincerity and appreciation are crucial. But it doesn't have to be anything difficult. Just give thought to your words, and rest assured that you're not the only person who has asked them before. But again, it's your gracious attitude and genuine appreciation that will make the difference.

Years ago, I got a cold call from a sales representative in the clothing business. She asked for a few minutes of my time to come in and show me her line of custom women's clothing. I wasn't sure if I was the custom-clothing type, but I said yes to the meeting. At the end of the meeting, I decided that I definitely was not the custom-clothing type of person and elected not to make a purchase. The meeting had been very pleasant and the sales representative had been gracious. Undaunted, she proceeded to what we are calling Question 4, but instead of asking, "Who else do you know that might be interested in buying from my line of custom clothing?" she asked slightly modified ones instead. Like, "Who do you know that is interested in fashion?" "Who do you know that you would describe as 'trendy'?" "Do you have any friends who drive fancy sports cars?" Had she asked me for a straight referral, I'm not sure I would have been able to deliver one. But with questions phrased in different ways, I was able to think of several possible names.

FIVE KEY QUESTIONS: QUESTION 5

Now, I know we've focused a lot on how to get what you need out of a networking meeting, but we can't lose sight of what networking really is—give-and-take. And while an entire book could be written about the give-and-take philosophy, this idea is worth repeating: Networking isn't all about you (or me). It's about *both* parties.

So, the last question you must ask in a networking meeting is:

"How can I help *you*?"

Yes, I admit that this question, given the topic of this book, might seem counterintuitive. But it's directly responsible for expanding your network and making evangelists of your contacts. In fact, it's possibly the most vital component of *The 20-Minute Networking Meeting*.

Big claims, right? Let me tell you why.

As we reminded ourselves above, networking isn't just about us, but about finding ways to help others, too. By nature, networking is something that benefits both parties. I mean, asking to network, receiving the gift of time, and asking for new contacts without offering something in return (even in spite of a gracious thank-you) is simply bad form. Worse, such a crime of *take, take, take* is rarely forgotten. But if you find a way to give back, you not only will be bestowed "good karma," you will demonstrate a clear indication of your consideration and appreciation for the time that was given to you. These days, that's not something for your contact to take lightly. Offering to help in a reciprocal way, too, creates a sense of a peer relationship. That's where you want to be.

Besides standing out from the pack, here's what such consideration and appreciation could get you:

→ Reciprocated respect and consideration (Who doesn't want to help someone who helps *them*?)

WHICH COULD LEAD TO:

→ An *additional* networking meeting with that contact

> → A meeting in a different part of the same organization

WHICH COULD LEAD TO:

→ An additional name that your contact was reluctant to give up at first (Sometimes networking contacts question whether they want to give away names, but gratitude and appreciation tip the scale.)

WHICH COULD LEAD TO:

→ A wider network (Translation: more word of mouth about *you*.) Which could lead to:

> → An evangelist

> → A consulting / part-time gig

> → A great reputation as a thoughtful businessperson

> → And the best of all: a job opportunity!

SO HOW DO YOU PHRASE THE QUESTION?

By saying it directly. "How can I help *you?*"

Of course it could be phrased a few other ways, too, but asking in an off-handed manner just doesn't come across as sincere, nor does it suggest actual consideration, wouldn't you say? And no one is going to be sincere with you if you're not sincere with them.

WHAT IF THEY'RE TAKEN BY SURPRISE?

This is sure to happen. As I mentioned, it's rare for people to offer help in return for help, right? Be prepared by having done your homework. Here are some scenarios:

> *"Thanks so much for the time and information you've given me, Sally. Now, how can I help you?"*

Sally gives you a look of shock.

> *"Gosh, Bill, I guess I can't think of anything at the moment."*

But, you know how important it is to give, and if you have done your homework, you'll know what to do.

What would that be, you ask? Read on for some possibilities:

- *"Well, you mentioned an interest in connecting with Dr. Ran Lee. I worked with him on my thesis. It's been a few years, but I would be happy to make the connection."*

- *"I am involved in planning the next event for our trade association. How about if I send over a free pass for you or someone on your team to attend the session?"*

- *"I saw that you are involved on the parks board. I teach playground safety courses. Could I contact someone there and volunteer to teach a course?"*

That's just to show a few. But if there seems to be nothing you could connect with right at that moment, have a backup:

"Well, Sally, I really appreciated your time and input. If you think of anything I can help with, I hope you'll give me a call. Still, as a token of appreciation for your time, I brought you a reprint of a Harvard Business School article on leadership in merging organizations. I thought you might find it interesting given your company's current M&A strategy."

NOTE: You could only pull something like that off if you've done your homework. If you don't know what's going on in your contact's organization, such a move is a lot less effective, or maybe ineffective. (Reminder: *Do your homework!*)

Over the years, networkers who get this have done many things for me in return. One person gave me information on a trade organization that I have since joined. A recent networking meeting resulted in a somewhat lopsided conclusion. I offered some suggestions to the job seeker on preparing a professional bio and an idea for a potential consulting gig. The person I was meeting with, on the other hand, offered me two contacts and also offered to recommend me to a somewhat elite women's leadership group!

SUMMARY

No matter whom you meet with, and no matter what you talk about, just end your meeting with Question 5.

Why end with it? Because you have an agenda to stick to, and this is the best place to ask this question. More importantly, it's what will leave your contact with a solid final impression of you should your meeting get interrupted or end early. Let it be one of consideration and appreciation—that you are gracious and grateful. Everyone is proud to know of such a thoughtful, considerate person, and better yet, everyone likes to help those people when possible.

REAL-WORLD PERSPECTIVE

Naomi, a public and corporate affairs executive for a Fortune 500 company, had the following reaction when a networker asked, "What can I do to help you?"

"I about fell out of my chair," she said. "No one had ever asked me that."

But the reciprocity and the power of that question didn't stop there. Allowing herself to accept the offer, the networking favor was returned.

"Knowing I might be leaving in a few months due to downsizing, I asked the person if they could connect me with someone at another organization. They did."

Many things changed after that day—including the fact that the original networker who requested to meet with Naomi "has been a valuable part of my network ever since."

And what about now?

"It was such a poignant moment for me when that question was asked," Naomi said, that she has continued the practice herself. The response she gets?

"The response is often a 'stunned silence.' And when I suggest a couple of ways (to help)—sending an article, helping them connect with someone in my network— the person opens up."

How's that for the power of offering to help in return? And that's coming from an executive whose expertise is media, government, and community communications!

THE IMPORTANCE OF GIVING

Then there's the flip side. While thinking about this book, and wanting to put its concept and message into practice, I agreed to meet with a C-level (chief executive/financial/operations) executive who requested a networking meeting with me. The person was referred by someone I respect, so I figured this was as solid a setup as I could ask for.

We made an appointment, and she arrived at the appropriate date and time. So far, so good. Then she jumped in by telling me about the types of jobs that she wanted. (Remember: Executive recruiters are not a grocery store, and we're not immediately your pathway to your next job. Executive recruiters operate in accordance with clients' hiring necessities, not a candidate's hiring desires.) I looked through her résumé and offered some recommendations and referrals, and very quickly, twenty minutes had elapsed.

Then, I turned the tides. I told her that, if we could, I was hoping the second part of the meeting could be about helping me. I told her I was interested in some leadership programs she had attended and some executive women's groups she belonged to. I wanted to spend a few minutes picking her brain about those topics for my benefit.

Well, despite the fact that this was a *networking* meeting (which means it goes both ways—give and take, remember), the meeting stopped cold. There was a look of almost shock on her face. She hadn't even considered the idea of mutuality or helping the other person. I kept my own questions brief, and the discussion continued cordially, but I learned something that day. Many folks in transition have still not picked up on the concept of giving back. My suggestion: Be different. Bring an attitude of helpfulness.

Turn to page 155 for examples of some actual items you might give as a token of your gratitude.

NEXT UP: STEP 4 — Great Ending

Step 4 —
Great Ending

GOAL:	Make a great final impression
TIME LIMIT:	2 minutes
WHAT YOU WILL DO:	Review any action, express more gratitude, *wrap it up*!

GREAT ENDING

Every great beginning has a great ending. Now that you have reviewed your background with your contact, managed the robust discussion between the two of you, and found a way to be helpful in return, you're ready to conclude the meeting.

At this point in your career, you know that there are a number of ways to signal that you are wrapping up the meeting. What's most important in this case is doing so in a clear manner.

: Your 20-minute networking meeting is probably shorter than what your contact was prepared for, which is to say that your contact, while appreciating your meeting management skills, still might be expecting a longer session. Be clear when the meeting is done.

Here are some examples:

"Thanks again, Carmen, for your time. I'm grateful for your thoughts."

"Well, I will let you get back to your workday, Reginald. Thanks so much for meeting with me."

"My time is up, Kendra. You've been so gracious. Thank you."

Just like any of the past examples, these wrap-ups can be modified to fit your style, so long as you hit the most critical point: showing your gratitude and sincere appreciation.

HOW TO DO IT

There are two quick steps to the great ending: recapping what you and your contact will do next, and saying *thank you* a final time.

FIRST: REVIEW ACTIONS

After you indicate that you are ending the meeting, you'll want to review any actions or next steps from the session. It'll sound something like these:

"Thanks for agreeing to introduce me to Paul. It will be great to finally meet him. Also, I'll send you an invitation to the next business owner's roundtable."

"Okay, I will send you that list of possible vendors tomorrow. I hope that it saves you some time. And, I really look forward to the chance to meet with your company's vice president of HR. Thanks for agreeing to set that up."

"Well, to recap: I will send an email with Dr. Washington's information. I will also forward the résumé of that programmer who would be great for your project work. And, I really am

grateful that you will keep your eyes and ears open for jobs or contract assignments for me."

Notice that they all express gratitude and address "next steps." Also note that they are clear indicators that the end of the meeting has come.

SECOND: EXPRESS MORE GRATITUDE

I know I've mentioned gratitude a lot over the course of this book, but I often find that it seems undervalued. Please don't make this mistake. People appreciate being appreciated. And in the end, it will matter.

Here are some things that you'll probably be thankful for:
- Their expertise
- Their time
- Their wisdom
- Their suggestions
- Their willingness to help you at all

How about a few examples in expressing more gratitude?

"Wow! I knew you were an expert in the printed coatings field, Lavon, but you even surpassed your great reputation! Thank you for all that you shared with me about the new processes. It was fascinating."

"I value your wisdom, Bryce. You gave me some real and somewhat difficult things to think about. Your thoughts will make me a better candidate when a job opportunity opens for me, and for that I am grateful."

"Gail, we went over by ten minutes and I am so appreciative of your willingness to take the extra time to tell me about

possible connections at your sister company in Wisconsin. What a coincidence that we have a second home near that facility. I will follow up as we discussed, and I will not forget your generosity in talking with me about it."

REAL-WORLD PERSPECTIVE

Networker Joel learned *The 20-Minute Networking Meeting* model and has added a new emphasis on gratitude and humility.

"My meetings went up a notch, to an eight or nine, just by being grateful," he explained after I asked how his new approach was working for him. "I put more focus on it now. Expressing appreciation to the person for their time and the interruption in their day seems to be well received. So does thanking them for their ideas, their attention—just about everything that seems relevant."

Since then, Joel has said that he has seen this pay off in more contacts and robust relationships with the networking contacts after the initial meetings.

"They can see that I get it," he said, referring to their networking together. "And that counts for a lot."

WRAP-UP

While we've made clear all the things you do in a good wrap-up, it doesn't mean it should turn into a long goodbye. Remember, leave them wanting more. A brief but positive goodbye is all you need, and you're all set. All done.

NEXT UP: STEP 5 — Great Follow-Up

Step 5 —
Great Follow-Up

GOAL:	Follow up after the meeting
TIME LIMIT:	Varies
WHAT YOU WILL DO:	Take prompt action to follow up after the meeting
NOTE:	Turn to page 162 for your Great Follow-Up Tracker

GREAT FOLLOW-UP

We're nearly at the end of our networking journey together. Even so, these final pages should not be overlooked. They are as vitally important as the networking meeting itself.

Following up is yet another way to show appreciation for your contact's gift of time. As important, it's also a way to start your future networking relationship. So what's involved in follow up? Here's a look.

WHAT TO DO: You should keep track of everything. *Everything*.

THE REASON: Keeping track of everything (in other words, keeping excellent notes) will allow you to back-reference your conversations, your communications, and any pertinent points of information that you should mention in your follow-up. Specific messages are far more appreciated than a simple thank-you and signature. Why? Because it leaves an impression of sincerity that you took your networking meeting to heart. Your solid notes will also help make your follow-up faster and more efficient. I mean, with everything already jotted down, you won't have to search your mind for thoughtful things to address in your follow-up, right?

◇◇◇

Keep track of *everything*. A solid set of notes will help you back-reference any pertinent points of information that you should mention in your follow-up.
It builds trust and a sense of reliability.
And follow-up is faster and more efficient.

◇◇◇

Here are some examples of what to keep track of. Be sure to write these things down the moment they happen!

- **Your phone calls.** If you speak with a contact by phone, write down the person's name and what you talked about (and that it was by phone). Keep track of things that strike you as important, new, or informative to your job search.

- **Your meeting dates.** Always be able to reference when you met, with whom you met, and what you talked about.
- **All correspondence.** Include time of original contact and responses.
- **Your follow-up messages.** (Yes, even your follow-up messages.) You should be able to look back at your notes and know that you followed up. Keeping track of your messages will also help you maintain a time line of correspondence. This will help you gauge when it's appropriate to reach out again in the future.
- **All other pertinent information** that you've learned along the way. There's no better way to make an evangelist out of a contact than having that person's points and information at your fingertips.

Does following up seem like a pain? Unnecessary? Just something you, or people you know, forget?

HERE ARE SOME PITFALLS TO AVOID:

"I will be employed soon. There won't be much need for follow-up because I will be in a new job before you know it."

WHY TO AVOID THIS MENTALITY: Though this could be the case, what if it doesn't happen as quickly as you expect? Building relationships (and getting on calendars) takes time. Take advantage of it. Prep and work as though the economy is in a recession and that jobs will be hard to come by. For any number of reasons, you may very well want this information months down the line.

"I've got a good memory. I don't need to track my fol-low-up communications, because I'll just remember it all."

WHY TO AVOID THIS MENTALITY: Networking can involve scores or even hundreds of people. Remembering dates, locations, topics, mutual connections, and personal or professional interests is going to become a major issue. Don't forget, when you meet a contact, all that person has to remember is *you* (which will be easy if you have a successful first meeting). How embarrassing would it be if you can't remember that person's suggestions and advice? Worse, if you can't remember the *person*?

"I'm more of a spontaneous worker. I'll just follow up on the fly."

WHY TO AVOID THIS MENTALITY: While many appreciate "living in the now," many also appreciate being remembered from the past. Take notes. Forgetting information that's important to your contact is just bad practice. Worse, it can damage trust and others' sense of your reliability. Instead, reinforce the positive perception that you create in your meetings by letting your contacts see you're taking notes. Allow yourself to be perceived as reliable by following up and referencing those notes. It will build trust, and that, along with reliability, is what builds evangelists.

REAL-WORLD PERSPECTIVE

A busy company president I know takes time frequently to meet with executives in transition. He appreciates getting a follow-up message right away.

"It is shocking to me that follow-up is often so slow," he told me, frustrated with each networking meeting that ends with no follow-up communication. "If I've set aside an amount of time to network with someone, I would hope that they could set aside enough time to follow up with me—and not after two weeks!"

THE KINDS OF FOLLOW-UP

Believe it or not, there are two kinds of follow-up. First, we'll deal with the immediate follow-up, and then we'll focus some attention on ongoing follow-up.

IMMEDIATE FOLLOW-UP

- First person to follow up with: the networking contact you just met with
- Second person to follow up with: the networking contact who referred you

HOW TO FOLLOW UP: By sending a thank-you. A hand-written note is always preferred, but an email will work too, so long as you do either one right away.

Here is an example of a follow-up note to a networking contact:

Dear Rhonda,

It was so nice to reconnect with you last Thursday. I appreciate your advice on my job-search strategy with small companies and your perspective on the overall venture-backed market.

Congratulations on the success your firm has had this year—great to read about your ten-year anniversary

celebration and your newest office. Finally, the picture of
your grandson was a hoot! Thanks for sharing it.

I'll let you know about the next family-business collab-
orative session. Look forward to seeing you there!

Kind regards,
Paul Lightnow

And another:

Dear Namhee,

Thank you for meeting with me on September 6. You
took the time to peek at my résumé, which was extra kind
of you. Your suggestions were really helpful and I will fol-
low up on every single one!

As I mentioned during our meeting, the state agency
that I work for has a board meeting on September 13.
After that date, I will be making the contacts we discussed
and I'll keep you posted.

Thanks again,
Barb Igo

YOUR REFERRING CONTACT

Thanking your contacts is always a must-do, but sending gratitude to the contact who referred you to your new contact is also
very important. Considering this is how a network is expanded,
and ultimately how work is obtained, it's an essential part of the
chain. Never forget to loop back to your referring contact with a
thank-you for the introduction to your new contact!

Here is an example of a loop-back thank-you message addressed
to your referring contact:

Dear Dale,

Thanks so much for your referral to Sherri Coyle. We met yesterday. Just as you said, Sherri is a top-notch marketing executive. She had some great ideas about the relative value of some of the professional certifications I am considering.

I really appreciated the chance to meet with you and Sherri and am grateful for your time and input.

Hopefully, our paths will cross at an upcoming Little League tournament. In the meantime, please let me know if there is anything I can do for you.

All the best,
Alec DeCalliz

Here's another example:

Dear Kathy,

Thanks so much for referring me to Alice Riggs. We met for coffee yesterday.

As you predicted, it was a great connection. Alice's business and mine are in complementary, but not overlapping, spaces. We may very well be able to refer projects to each other in the future. We also discovered a mutual fondness for hiking and wine tasting!

Thanks again. I look forward to seeing you soon. You mentioned valuing some input on your client proposals. Don't hesitate to let me know if I can assist you with that.

Kind regards,
Blake Reed

ONGOING FOLLOW-UP

So, what is ongoing follow-up, if not continued contact? Well, it's actually networking maintenance. Many times executives send their thanks and gratitude and think that's that. This is acceptable, but it doesn't help expand or strengthen their network.

So how does one continue to follow up, you ask? And how often is appropriate? These are common questions, and the answers are pretty straightforward. Read on.

WHEN TO BE IN TOUCH

- **If you find an article or website** that you genuinely think the person would value. Don't ever forward something meaningless just to send a follow-up message. It can backfire. But thoughtful information, sent with good wishes and a brief update, may be welcome.
- **If your contact information has changed.** For example, if you have moved or have a new phone number or email address, you should reconnect with your network to inform them of the change. Attach an updated résumé to an email message if you're still in transition.
- **If your employment status has changed,** or if you have

completed a degree or earned a significant certification. Again, you should attach an updated résumé if you are still in job-search.

Examples:

Suzy,

Thanks again for meeting with me and for being a part of my network. I wanted to update you that I have completed both my project management certificate and my MBA in operations leadership from the University of St. Ambrose. Yeah!! I value our connection and I look forward to staying in touch. Please let me know if you hear of any related consulting projects or if I can help you in any way.
Pedro

Additional reasons for ongoing follow-up:

- **If you are thinking about the person and want to say hello.** Sometimes a nicely worded message to say hi is okay, but it should not be done too often; it can be perceived more as social or even bothersome and not professional. Use judgment.
- **If your networking introduces you to someone** who is closely connected with your contact. People enjoy it when a mutual connection is shared. When the world becomes smaller, trust is built. A word of advice, though: you should be sure about the relationship. I've had plenty of people call me and proudly tell me that they were referred to me by a "friend" of mine. Unfortunately, I frequently don't know the supposed "friend" who has connected us.
- **If you want to further discuss something mentioned in**

the meeting. Perhaps your meeting revealed that you and your contact are both watching a certain start-up company or the publication of a new book by an author in your field.

How about:

Kelly,

Thanks again for meeting with me a few weeks ago. I hope you had a fantastic Fourth of July! In case you didn't catch this article about LTEX in the Corporate Journal, I've attached a copy. Just as we thought! They have both production lines up and running! Your advice was much appreciated. Please let me know if I can ever be of assistance to you.
Tim Naylor

One more:

- **If you have news to share** about someone you both know (a promotion, new company, an award, etc.).

Margarethe,

It was such a treat spending time with you last month. I am in final interviews with two corporations, so I hope I will be making an announcement to you soon! In the meantime, I wanted to let you know that our mutual friend Solara has won the state Business Start-up Award! I'm sending along a flyer about the celebration event. I hope that you, or someone on your team, can attend.
Kind regards,
Loretta Stein

WHAT TO DO: If you have meaningful reasons to check back or update a contact or contacts, then do so! Professional judgment is a must here, of course. You don't want to call every three weeks just to shoot the breeze. But you don't want to disappear, either.

◇◇

Unless you have an update including time-sensitive or significant information, consider staying in touch about once a quarter, at most. Every few weeks is too often!

◇◇

THE KIND OF FOLLOW-UP YOU DON'T DO

- **Mass emails** where the email addresses of all parties are visible. (This one is horrible. It is impersonal. It also shows just how many people you're not taking seriously.) Instead, take the time to personalize each message. After all, people have networked with you one-on-one, so stay in touch in the same way.
- **Too-frequent updates** with only minuscule changes in your situation to report.
- **Stories, quotes, or platitudes** about general topics. Some job-searchers who have run out of meaningful professional updates turn to sending generic bits about leadership or business strategy, hoping that they will be noticed and remembered. After a fashion, these types of messages, if not automatically deleted, are remembered for the wrong reasons.

In our office we value meaningful updates from people we know. We share pertinent information about people among ourselves and put the most current information into our database. On the other hand, we joke about the silly, meaningless updates we get from other folks. How would *you* react to a weekly email from a job seeker containing jokes, song lyrics, philosophical quotes, ditties, and the like?

EXAMPLES OF GOOD AND BAD FOLLOW-UP

First, a good follow-up message:

Hi Jan,

Thanks again for meeting with me last month. I hope you are enjoying the nice weather.

How about this for a coincidence? I connected with your former boss, Irwin Plank, at a chamber of commerce luncheon in Atlanta on Monday. I was there with a professional friend who has done some training for me over the years. Irwin had nothing but positive things to say about you and your time working together; he called them the "glory days" and said that you were the person he looked to for "voice of the client" insights. He asked me to send you his greetings.

I hope our paths cross again soon. In the meantime, please don't hesitate to let me know if I can ever help you in any way. You were amazingly helpful to me.

Best regards,

JaNae Hawes

Here's an example of a bad follow-up message:

Dear Colleagues,

 I have still not found a job. I want you all to continue to keep me in mind and refer me if you hear of openings such as director or vice president of administration.

 Or, you can forward my résumé to others who can help me.

 I am hearing about openings, but I'm just not "getting up to the plate." Why not??
Sincerely,
Charly Bartels

Another bad follow-up message:

TO: *Mailing List*
SUBJECT: *"Ginny's Giant Leadership Tips, Volume XII"*

April is upon us, and I have the following quotes for you:

"The way to do is to be." —Lao Tzu
"People should not consider so much what they are to do, as what they are." —Meister Eckhart

I'm thinking about a lot these days and I hope you are all thinking about me!
Sincerely,
Ginny St. Charles

And of course, what will happen if you don't follow up at all: This might sound harsh, but you'll be forgotten. If you don't stay in touch in some way, people will assume you have landed in a new job and will not continue to think of you. But, again, what you don't want to do is follow up so frequently that you become a bother. It's about balance. People who have taken the time to meet with you are people who care about you. Honor both their time and their concern with meaningful, occasional updates.

REAL-WORLD PERSPECTIVE: JIM

Jim is a business unit president at a large manufacturing corporation. When asked why he stopped accepting networking requests, this is what he had to say.

"The reason I quit accepting requests for meetings with people in transition is that I got sick of feeling used. Over the years I have met with dozens of people looking for a new job.

"I'm the head of a business unit in a large manufacturing company that has been voted one of our state's best places to work for five years in a row. It is totally understandable why people would want to network their way into our company. It is indeed a great place to work.

"But here's what has bothered me. I would take the time to meet with people, then I would never hear another word. Nothing. No thank-you, no follow-up, no nothing. The worst part is seeing a notice on LinkedIn or a trade publication that the person landed in a new job months ago, and me not knowing anything about it. I'd like to feel that my small contribution somehow helped them land in a job. Maybe that's just conceit. But how long does it take to send a quick email thanking people? How long does it take to prepare and send an announcement? How long to call with a message? Certainly, less time than I took for a meeting to help you when you needed it!

"Sorry to be so rigid about it. But that is my experience. I have heard the same from other execs at my company. So I quit accepting these meetings altogether. I refer callers to our HR department instead."

NEXT UP: Pulling It All Together

Pulling It All Together

We're nearing the end of our *20-Minute Networking Meeting* journey. We've enjoyed laying out the model for you, and we hope you can see ways to put it into practice for your own job search. We have seen these techniques succeed time and time again and have witnessed the incredible results: better meetings, better impressions, more evangelists, more opportunities, better and sooner employment.

As we cruise the home stretch, let's look at what Ione, an administrative vice president and convert to *The 20-Minute Networking Meeting* concepts, had to say about her experience. One of the first to try out the system, she gave us this feedback: *"Overall, it has worked great! It's been far easier than I thought it would be."*

Hoping for more specifics, I asked her what she had done differently than in the past.
"When I got to a meeting, instead of just jumping right in, I started by reminding the person who I was and how we were connected. In some cases, it had been several weeks since we had set up the meeting, and I couldn't really expect people to remember who had referred me. That was a smart move. Reminding them was helpful, as they didn't seem to have a starting point with me until that

moment. What I noticed is that it kick-started my conversations because we suddenly had something to talk about."

What next?
"It took some practice, but now I'm better at keeping the ball rolling. In meetings, I go over my background with much less detail than I used to. Less is more! I got more attention, more relevant questions, more thoughtful discussion."

I asked Ione why she thought that was.
"I think it was just easier for my contacts to keep track of my career path. At first, I thought I would feel cheated by a more abbreviated discussion time, but keeping it brief seemed to pay off much more. I think that was because it left room for discussion about what I had briefed them on. The expanded discussions told me I was making a better impression."

I asked what else was different from what she'd done before.
"Asking for additional contacts. I do that now. I hated the idea of doing it at first, and it's still a little strange, but no one seems surprised. I mean—it's networking. These days, I don't shy away from the question at all. Every networking meeting has generated about three new contact names, I would say, which of course results in more meetings and more names. My network has expanded exponentially, and I feel like I'm really 'getting the lay of the land' when it comes to my industry. In fact, because of this, it has even changed my thoughts about my career path, mostly because of what I've learned along the way. I couldn't have done that without so many conversations about the market and getting so many diverse perspectives—all for asking for more people to talk with."

How do the meetings end? I wondered if that was any different.

"It's quick now. I used to say long goodbyes. I think that's because I felt so indebted for their time. But now my wrap-up is confident and succinct. I've realized this has also been well received. Maybe because it leaves the impression that I'm sensitive to the person's time. Someone even told me they wished everyone could 'stick to the ropes' the way I had."

And the follow-up?

"I try to get it done right away. It feels like if I wait more than a day, my follow-up could come across like an after-thought. I don't want to risk that."

What do you do for the follow-up?

"It's usually an email, but sometimes I send a greeting card or small gift, if the person was particularly helpful. But most importantly, I just follow up quickly."

I asked whether anyone had commented on how she approached the networking meeting.

"Actually, after my last networking meeting, the person I was sitting with commented on how well I had managed our time together. To think that I used to take more time than this. And to think I've sat with people who took more time than twenty minutes. It's just a lot easier this way. And much more appreciated."

One Final Example

A Sample 20-Minute Networking Meeting

L et's take one last look at the principles of *The 20-Minute Networking Meeting* in action. The following pages contain a full example of what a networking meeting looks like. You can understand, of course, that your meetings won't go exactly as this one does, but you'll get the gist of how things might work, and, more importantly, why they work that way.

We'll follow the example with imagined Q&A sheets with our imaginary characters, and give example takeaways that point out the lessons. Enjoy!

SAMPLE 20-MINUTE NETWORKING MEETING

The following scenario shows the networking interaction between John Olvera, a recently laid-off executive, and Walt Lee, a professional with whom John serves on a nonprofit board.

JOHN OLVERA & WALT LEE

John pushed back his chair and stood up. Another productive board meeting completed. He was proud to be associated with this organization. Although it had been many years since his mother had died from heart disease, being on the board of the state's Heart Disease Foundation made him feel like he was doing something in her memory.

John compiled his papers from the meeting and put them in his folio. As he left the conference room, he heard his name called out. Waiting for him outside was Walt Lee, a fellow board member.

"More board business?" John asked Walt.

"No, we've had plenty of that today," Walt said. "But I heard that you were affected by the merger at AEB. How are you doing?"

John still wasn't comfortable talking about this.

"Doing all right," he replied, despite feeling the opposite. Truth was, being between jobs was eating at him. At the country club, he had avoided the topic entirely when Howard asked the same thing. But in retrospect, John felt ridiculous. Howard could have been helpful.

"Any luck?" Walt asked as they waited for an elevator.

This was as good a time as any. It had never been easy for John to ask for help, but fortune wasn't going to drop in his lap, and if he kept it up, his pride was going to keep him out of work.

"No, nothing new," John replied. "But I'm starting to network. Trying to make some headway." Now was the hard part. "And I would actually value a few minutes of your time and wisdom if you'd lend it to me. Twenty minutes, no more."

He hit the elevator button. The reflection off the polished door showed apprehension on Walt's face, but it was gone when he turned to face John.

"Twenty minutes? Geez, I've got more time than that, John."

"You with work, me finding work, we're all busy," John said, sensitive to that fact. "Just twenty minutes. No more."

Walt grinned. This was new coming from John. Typically, John loved to cover the whole spectrum of business, something Walt appreciated about him.

"I'd be happy to," Walt replied. The elevator arrived. "I don't know if you recall," Walt continued as they stepped in, "but I was in your exact position this time last year."

John felt his eyebrows rise. Being so caught up in his own transition, he completely forgot about that. Looking back, he recalled Walt having a pretty tough time, just as he was now. It gave John a slight feeling of relief. He wasn't the only person to have been in this position. In fact, now he even had a feeling of hope; if Walt was able to go from unemployment to his current role as chief marketing officer, there was something to look forward to. Walt would have a lot to offer when they met up again.

"I appreciate it, Walt. I really do. I'll send you an email to set things up."

If I'd known it was this easy, John thought as he left the building, I'd have started weeks ago. But better late than never.

Two weeks later, John arrived at Walt's office with plenty to talk about. It seemed inconceivable to show up asking for leads with no ideas of his own, so he had done his homework.

Don't make Walt run the meeting, he told himself. He's not the one looking for a new opportunity.

"Come on in!" Walt said, shaking John's hand and gesturing toward a nearby conference room. John smiled. He couldn't recall Walt being this enthusiastic or happy. Something had gone right in this last year.

The two took seats at the conference room table. John set down his coffee cup and his belongings. He felt humbled asking for Walt's time, and wanted to stick to his promise of twenty minutes.

"Thanks again for meeting with me, Walt. I appreciate it."

"No problem, John. It's great to see you. Besides, I also wanted to ask you a quick question about our board governance committee meeting two weeks ago."

As usual, Walt got right down to business. The two had started their board membership together a few years ago, and there was always plenty to discuss. But after a few minutes of recap, John retook the lead, telling himself to keep to his word: twenty minutes. With a smile—and a much more comfortable feeling—he began.

"I noticed that besides the board, you manage the youth hockey league with my neighbor Matt Meek." Matt was a nice guy, and the person who reminded John to talk to Walt. "That makes you a pretty busy guy."

Walt laughed. "True. A busy sport, hockey."

John moved forward with his agenda. He couldn't jump right into it though, without giving Walt a bit of a lead-up. "What I'd like to do, Walt, is tell you a bit about my background and situation. Then, if it's okay, I have a couple of topics that I would value your perspective on.

"As you know, I got caught up in the merger of AEB and Stevensco. I was a US regional vice president there—AEB—and my background has mostly been in medical device manufacturing and some audio components manufacturing as well. But I started as an electrical engineer—too many years ago to mention—and I've been in general management since then, for about the last fifteen years. Ideally, I'd like to stay in a leadership role in a distributed manufacturing company of any size. That could be medical devices, but I'm open to anything that has growth potential."

Walt nodded, reflecting on what John had said. Just to clarify, John added:

"Just let me be clear, Walt: I'm not asking you to find me any kind of job. All I'm trying to do is familiarize myself with the territory and learn a bit from your experience." This is where his homework came into play. "For instance, would you tell me more about your company's new product initiatives? I've done some reading, and it seems like the focus is on acquiring and growing related small businesses." Walt nodded and John followed up. "From my past work, I happen to know that a couple of these acquired organizations are specifically related to manufacturing facilities. Have you been involved in any of these businesses? Are there any changes or trends that affect the types of companies that I might be connecting with?"

John could see it: This question caused a change in Walt's expression. Something clicked, and ideas were forming in his mind.

Walt responded briefly about what he knew, and mentioned that a couple of the businesses were taking a new direction, while another was expanding its current efforts. For John, this was a major eye-opener and he jotted down the information. Regretting not having done this already, he made sure not to miss a single thing.

After another question about Walt's perception on an industry certification course, John decided to ask for a couple more thoughts—this time on Walt's own transition experience. After all, what better person to ask than someone who had already traveled the road?

"Last time we saw each other, Walt, you mentioned having been in transition. To be honest, I had completely forgotten about that, but I'd appreciate hearing a thing or two you know now that you wish you'd known then."

Walt grinned, surprising John.

"You bet."

Walt sat forward on his seat. John was asking him questions

that he should have asked others while *he* was out of work. Walt saw this as wise, and was more than happy to share that wisdom. Had he gotten such thoughts a year ago, it wouldn't have taken him nearly as long to get a new job.

"I wish I had known how valuable my time in transition would be," Walt said regretfully. "And I wish I would have enjoyed it more instead of being so consumed with the fact that I lost my job." He picked up his coffee and leaned back in his seat. "See— and I'm not proud to admit this, you understand—it took me a while to network. But what I realized, very late in the game, was that I could have been having fun at the same time. Once I started networking, I realized that it was nice to see old friends and colleagues and that I could have done all that much, much earlier on. Now that I look back, I probably could have gotten work much earlier as a result."

John nodded. He respected Walt, and he wouldn't take his words for granted. Thankfully, he hadn't let too much time get away from him before starting his networking. After all, if Walt had a difficult time getting a job without networking, John was sure it was not going to be any easier for him.

"What did the networking do for you? I mean besides, you know, helping get you a job?"

"For starters, I have new friendships," Walt replied. "And I've renewed old ones. And it's helped my professional work because after meeting as many new people as I did, I developed a wide network that I'm able to use for business and a variety of other things. Really, I should have been doing it while I was employed, too. But now, I guess I am, like sitting with you."

John smiled. Pearls of wisdom. Wisdom that was really common sense. Yet he had been ignoring it all this time.

Walt's response hit near John's next question. It was the toughest of them all, but he reminded himself that Walt, along with hundreds of others like him, probably had asked the same one.

"You said you developed a wide network, Walt," John said. "That you kept meeting new people. I'm hoping to do the same—develop a wide network and meet new people. Do you know others I could connect with as part of my job search? Maybe people who have done some of the start-up work we talked about?"

John braced for the worse. It used to make him uncomfortable to answer such a question, but this was coming from a place of honesty and sincerity, so he could only be gracious if he was denied.

"I just might," Walt said. "I have a couple of contacts in my C-level roundtable with medical device background. I'm not sure if they're going to lead you right to a new job, but they're well connected, too, and have a pretty good feel for the medtech sector." He smiled and wrote two names on a piece of paper.

"Is it all right that I use your name?"

"Yes, but just know that the second person is someone I'm still getting to know. But I trust you, John, and I know you'll do right by him."

John smiled and began putting his things back into his portfolio.

"One more question, Walt. How can I help *you*?"

Walt sat quietly. Obviously he wasn't expecting the question.

"Well, I can't think of anything, John. You're doing great work on our board projects."

"Well, please think about it," John replied. "You're active with the Humane Society. Maybe I can offer you a helping hand there." John stood and held out his hand as he spoke. "And you're still a big golfer, right . . . ?"

"Where you going?" Walt interrupted as he stood up with him. John had told him ahead of time that he would only be twenty minutes, but Walt was still taken by surprise. *Everyone* said twenty minutes.

"A promise is a promise. I said twenty minutes. I really appreciate your insights and your referrals, Walt, but I really mean to let you get back to your day."

Walt shook John's hand. He was a very different man than the last time they'd met, but now Walt had an even deeper appreciation for John's professionalism. He was clearly very serious about getting his next opportunity.

"I'm certainly glad I could help. I think we covered some good ground in just twenty minutes," Walt responded.

"Before I go," John said, opening his briefcase. "I wanted to give this to you as a token of thanks." He handed Walt a book about training black labs. "The last time we talked," he explained, "you mentioned your interest in dog training. I happened to see this book, and given our conversation at the time, thought you might like what the author has to say."

Walt beamed as he thumbed through the book. It was a big expression of thanks, especially since he hadn't expected anything at all. More impressive was that John had remembered something that was dear to Walt—sporting dogs had been part of his family for generations.

"It's kind of you, John. Thank you."

"And when the Humane Society has its annual golf event," John said, picking up his earlier thought, "please let me know. I'll put together a foursome from my club to help out. Otherwise, I'll be in touch again after I've met with your colleagues. Thanks again, Walt."

Q&A with John Olvera: "How did it go for you?"

What did you do to plan for *The 20-Minute Networking Meeting*?

I looked Walt up on LinkedIn and was surprised by what I didn't know about him. Walt is connected to my neighbor Matt through youth hockey. I happened to ask Matt about Walt, and Matt reminded me to talk to Walt. Also, Walt is a past participant in an industry leadership certification program that I might be interested in—another great thing to talk about when we meet up again.

How did the meeting itself go for you?

I liked it. I liked knowing that I felt respected for staying on track, too. In a way, he seemed to really respect that I was keeping to my word. Better yet, I got all the information I needed to continue my networking, and I have a feeling of optimism that I can do this.

Was twenty minutes long enough?

Definitely! Walt was actually the person asking for more time! I was still able to tell Walt about my background and what I was looking for, and ask for his thoughts on transition and networking. In that time, we were also able to cover a couple of quick board issues. I told him that I was going to stick to twenty minutes, and I did!

What do you think Walt got out of it?

A new respect for me. I know he's been in this position, and I know that he knows it's hard. Seeing that I was willing to ask for help was a big deal. Also, before the meeting, I think Walt probably thought I wanted to stay with a big company. Telling him I was open to a small or mid-size company was probably something he didn't know. It was good to clarify that point. It opens my chances up for more work. And overall, I think he got a better understanding of my expertise.

How do you plan to follow up?

I plan to send Walt an email today, thanking him for his time. He's a great guy. I might also reiterate my willingness to help with the golf benefit. I'll definitely let him know when I've made contact with the folks he referred me to. He should know that I took advantage of what he offered me, and that I didn't waste his twenty minutes.

Is there anything you would do differently next time?

I'll stay more open about these meetings. I won't be as nervous about them. Only good things could come out of them—definitely nothing bad. At the very worst, nothing will happen.

Q&A with Walt Lee: "How did it go for *you?*"

What did you like about John's *20-Minute Networking Meeting*?

John and I have known each other for a while, but I like that he was still sensitive about my time. So many networking meetings are just long sessions that don't get to the point. Maybe it's because it feels good to be in something like a business meeting, I don't know. But that's no excuse for disrespecting the time of others, and John didn't do that.

He was also prepared with things to discuss, and he knew a lot about my company. And he treated the meeting seriously; it wasn't just for chitchat. He had thought ahead of time about what I could add to his job search, and he had some good questions lined up. I liked that. Plus, he brought me a book about dogs. That was not necessary, but thoughtful. I can't believe he remembered that conversation. Now I'll remember that he remembered.

Was it long enough?

Actually, not quite. I was literally left wanting more. I like John and would have enjoyed talking to him for a little while longer, but I know he's serious about his job hunt, and I'm sure he knew I was busy, too. If he gets back to me about how his meetings go with the contacts I set him up with, we'll probably get more time to catch up. Besides, I'm going to forward his information to another guy I know. We'll probably end up talking about that, too, maybe after a board meeting.

Were you expecting anything that didn't happen in this meeting?

I was expecting it to be longer and I was expecting it to be less structured. Networking meetings seem to be conversations where people want to just chat—a get-to-know-you session. This was different, and it threw me, but in a good way. John had a plan, which he stuck to, and he actually led the meeting. That was a first. I was surprised that all I had to do was sit back and help when I could. Which is the whole point, I suppose. Now I've learned something, too.

Is there anything you would change about the meeting?

Well, there is nothing I can think of that I would change about this meeting, in particular. But, I suppose there might need to be a little flexibility at times. If I was meeting with a former coworker I had not seen in twenty-five years, we might need more than twenty minutes to catch up! On the other hand, I suppose the catching up part could be separate. We could catch up for a while, then move into the networking meeting. But I'd like it if there was some give and take there.

The End

Surprised to suddenly find yourself at the end? Don't be. You now have all the tools necessary for a new—and different—kind of job search. Take time to hone them. Make them yours. While it was our intent to create a simple and straightforward model incorporating the best of what we have seen in the most effective networking meetings, it will be up to you to personalize your style and make things work in your favor. All it takes is the commitment and desire to make it happen. And, as you know, these are things you've already mastered as an executive.

As we part ways (for now), here are a few things to remember.

- **Networking is more than important; it is vital.** It is the lifeblood of your job search.

- **Networking meetings don't have to be complicated.** Your simple objectives for each meeting are to learn a little, gain an additional contact or two, and, hopefully, create an evangelist. If it doesn't happen in one meeting, try to make it happen at the next. That's it.

- **Networking meetings have a beginning, middle, and end.** Remember that since you called the meeting, it will be up to you to manage where the meeting stands. Be clear about the start and, once you've finished your brief and meaningful discussion, be clear about the end.

- **Throughout each of your discussions, you will be displaying your preparedness,** your organizational skills, your focus, and your genuine interest in the other person. Make it count. How well you do this will define the impression that you leave your contact with.

- **Networking is give-and-take!** Reciprocate, and always be prepared with something to give back.

- *You have flexibility.* We are fully aware that we've built a "networking model," but truth be told, the model won't work without some room to move. Use judgment. If your meeting lasts twenty-five minutes, no problem! If your session ends at eighteen minutes, no problem! Simply use it as a guide.

That's it. *Fin! Finito!* The world is now your oyster. Take it. Own it. Make it yours! We wish you the best as you hit the networking circuit and hope that your new experiences show immediate and permanent changes to your career objectives. Have faith. And trust. Without a doubt, positive change will come, and with it, the next chapter of your career!

APPENDIX

Your 20-Minute Networking Meeting Cheat Sheet

Print or tear this page out. Mark it. Use it as a guideline. Pace your house and be sure you know its order and its content. Once you have it locked down, figure out where there can be flexibility, and allow yourself to develop it.

Congratulations on finishing *The 20-Minute Networking Meeting*. Now go get started!

STEP 1:	Great First Impression
TIME LIMIT:	*2–3 minutes: thanks and chitchat*
STEP 2:	Great Overview
TIME LIMIT:	*1 minute overview of experience*
STEP 3:	Great Discussion
TIME LIMIT:	*12–15 minutes: 5 key questions*
STEP 4:	Great Ending
TIME LIMIT:	*2 minutes: thanks and wrap-up*
STEP 5:	Great Follow-Up
TIME LIMIT:	*Meaningful follow-up, right after the meeting*

The Readiness Exercise

*(Or: Take This Little Test to
See If You're Ready)*

Take twenty minutes to answer the following questions. Think through each answer before you write. This is not a race. It's about bringing focus to what you don't know about yourself yet. The purpose is to help you get grounded in what you bring to the market and to each networking interaction. These questions can be used as an indicator of your readiness to step back into the job market. Don't stop here, however. You can continue to learn the steps of your 20-minute networking meeting, but be sure you have solid answers to the following questions before you begin any actual networking. Good luck!

The Readiness Exercise

1. What aspects of your work are you really, really good at? For guidance: What gets you the most compliments? What did your boss rate you highest on? What do you do faster, better than others?

_____

_____

_____

_____

2. What personality traits do you bring to the workplace? What characteristics have been praised by others? What aspects of your style have been particularly valued? Now is probably a great time to dust off any personality or leadership-style inventories or assessments you may have taken in the past. If you don't have a recent assessment, it would be a good idea to take one or more now. Alternatively, you could ask some of your evangelists or former coworkers for their perspective on this question. (_Don't be afraid to ask. They'll see that you're doing the kind of homework that you should be doing._)

_____

_____

_____

_____

3. What areas of specific expertise do you have that others don't?

_____

_____

_____

_____

4. What else makes you a unique executive? (International experience; special training or certifications; board memberships; having survived times of fast growth, turnarounds, mergers; etc.)

_____

_____

_____

_____

5. Complete the following sentence:

"An organization would be fortunate to have me join them as

(*job role*)_____

because _____

_____

_____

_____

_____."

6. Respond to the following sentence: "Even though the above is true, I am still working on developing myself in the following areas." (*This is where the perspectives of former coworkers come in handy.*) _____

_____

_____

_____

_____

_____

_____

_____

_____

7. I am highly confident I am going to come out of this transition okay.
☐ Yes   ☐ No

8. I have the resources to make this transition a great experience.
☐ Yes   ☐ No

DONE. Now take a ten-minute break and review your answers. Do they reflect what you *really* think and feel? Being sure you are rock-solid with these answers is what's going to give you confidence in your networking meetings. Don't rush it. And come back to this worksheet and revise your answers as you find a better way to express yourself.

The Great First Impression Planner

Here's a quick worksheet to help you figure out your game plan and to make a solid first impression. Feel free to tear this out and fill it in if that's best for you.

WHAT YOU'RE GOING TO DO:

Take twenty minutes to answer these questions after setting up a meeting. Recheck your responses for any opportunity to tweak the answers or strengthen your information.

- **Arrival** *(Early, but not **too** early!)*
- **Where are we meeting?** *(Make sure this is established.)*
- **What's the address?** *(Make sure you're sure.)*
- **Do I know how to get there?** *(Be darned positive. You don't want to be late due to construction, weather, traffic, location parking, flat tire, or the odd traffic ticket.)*

FIRST IMPRESSIONS

If meeting at the contact's office, do I know the dress code, if any?

☐ Yes   ☐ No

(If in doubt, ask a colleague or someone at the office's front desk. Better yet, come dressed professionally. If you're a job-seeker, the last impression you want to leave is that you were more casually dressed than your contact.)

Do I know how to pronounce the contact's name correctly?

☐ Yes   ☐ No

(Boy, do we see and hear this one a lot. It's hard to help someone who doesn't even know your name. It's also hard to get past the embarrassment when you screw it up.)

SETTING THE AGENDA

Have you planned your agenda?

☐ Yes   ☐ No

Do you know your five key questions? *(Go back to Step 3 — Great Discussion if you don't recall this part.)*

☐ Yes   ☐ No

HIGHLIGHTING CONNECTIONS

Have I done my homework in order to make great connections?

☐ Read the contact's company website

☐ Read any personal bios available on the organization's website

☐ Reviewed contact's LinkedIn profile; noted any connections in common

☐ Did a Google search; noted any outside board positions; interests; things in common; etc.

☐ Jotted down key connections to mention in your *20-Minute Networking Meeting*

The One-Minute
Overview Planner

O kay, here's how you put together your one-minute overview.

WHAT TO DO:

- **Print a copy of your résumé**
- **Decide what stands out**
- **Mark or highlight those items** (You'll be highlighting the most important features of your background that make you unique in your work.)
- **Find seven to ten things in total** (Shoot for five at the very least.) Here are some possibilities:
  - Your current position
  - Size and scope of your current responsibilities
  - What your current organization does (if not well-known)
  - Your prior position or positions, summarized

NOTE: This list is meant to *complement* Step 2 — Great Overview, not replace it. Use that Chapter to build your Great Overview, and use this list to augment it.

WHAT TO DO NEXT:

- Compile these key points on another document.
- Read through the points out loud.
- Time it. If it takes around one minute out loud, perfect; you've got your one-minute overview. If you're over, trim the fat and keep the most important points.
- If you're too short of a minute, add another point or leave it as-is if you feel good about it.
- Finally, string it all together using your own words (also known as "making it yours"). Take your time. Make it fluid and easy to understand. Done.

A QUICK REVIEW

Here, reworded, is the structure for your One-Minute Overview:

- Think about your number of years in the function
- Then think about the highlights of your background
- Follow with the places you've worked
- Tie them in with the most recent titles you've held

Now string them all together in a sentence or two (three or more will work, too—just stick with one minute). *Voilà!* One-minute overview!

TIP

Don't feel like you have to nail this thing in an afternoon. As you continue to work on your networking game plan, come back to it and rehearse it a few more times. This will help you learn your material in a natural way, rather than forcing the words to come out like a business pitch. Again, *make it your own*, and don't force anything.

Your Small Token of Gratitude

(Actual Things You Can Give in Return)

The consummate giver in my own network is our colleague Lars, a man who is 100% focused, 24/7, on what he can give to others. He has been cited as the "Most Networked Person in the Twin Cities" by the publication *Minnesota Business*. Lars is mid-30s and the most networked person because other people like knowing him. And they like knowing him because he is a giver at all levels.

Lars shared his philosophy of giving as a strategy for job seekers. Here is a thank-you note that he received (printed with his permission, with names changed to protect anonymity):

Hi, Lars:

I accepted a position at XYZ Corporation and start my new job on Monday! You can read the story in the business publication, but basically I'll be running their national sales and operations. It's a tremendously exciting opportunity and I'm just thrilled (and they are pretty happy, too).

I wanted to send you a heartfelt letter of thanks. You were perhaps the most influential person in my search, which found its true spark when we had coffee together. The idea of using this time to give back was the thesis statement of the last four months. I met more people, had more interesting meetings, made more of a difference, and was happier and more satisfied because of that advice.

My life has been measurably improved and it came from that simple thought: Don't think of what your network can do for you, think about what you can do for your network. And you were the person who sparked that idea, so I owe you a big thank-you.
Signed,
Executive Candidate

There you have it. Giving back works, and will work wonders for you, too.

Here are a few things you can give your contact in return. It never has to be anything big—just something that shows your appreciation.

- **Contact names.** This is a great one. Think about people in your own network that your contact might want to meet, and offer to make introductions.
- **Information.** Find up-to-date information on this person's industry or functional area and take articles, website addresses, or other sources to the meeting. If your research uncovers this person's hobbies or interests (such as animal rights, environmentalism, or the clarinet), take related contacts, connections, articles, websites, etc.

- **Potential client ideas.** If the person is a consultant, or related in any way to sales or marketing, he or she would likely be very appreciative of any ideas or referrals that you might have for possible clients. Even if your referral doesn't pan out in a sale, it will still be appreciated.
- **An actual gift.** Order fifty copies of your current favorite leadership book or article and take a copy to each of your networking meetings. Or, follow up by sending a plant, or a gift card to a coffee chain. Maybe executive luggage tags. Gourmet chocolates. We've received everything from restaurant gift cards and children's toys (it's a long story) to decorative mini-art pieces and invitations to interesting professional and cultural events. The sky's the limit here. (But don't feel obligated to buy a trick pony or cruise tickets. Nothing huge!)

TIP

Ultimately, your small token of gratitude could be part of Question 5 in Step 3 ("How can I help *you*?"). More specifically, if your contact is caught by surprise and hasn't given thought as to how you could return the gift of time, your token of gratitude would work well here. Alternatively, your small token of gratitude could be something you send at a later time, too. But not too late—you wouldn't want your contact to feel like an afterthought. Be prompt!

The Great Discussion Planner

This section is a summary of the five key questions. Using it, take twenty minutes to plan a great discussion, and use it as a quick reference for future conversations.

QUESTIONS 1–3
(THREE UNIQUE QUESTIONS)

Think about what you know of this networking contact. What information is this person uniquely able to give you? The questions are structured as follows:

> **Fact about Contact (Observation)**
> *followed by*
> **Follow-Up Question (Related Question)**

Here are the breakdowns, followed by their full approaches:

EXAMPLE 1:

Fact about Contact (Observation):
Your company was recently acquired by 3M.

Follow-Up Question (Related Question):
How have you found the transition to a larger organization?

Full Approach:
"Your company was recently acquired by 3M. How have you found the transition to a larger organization?"

EXAMPLE 2:

Fact about Contact (Observation):
You graduated from the Leaders of Tomorrow program.

Follow-Up Question (Related Question):
Was that a valuable program to you in your career? In what way?

Full Approach:
"You graduated from the Leaders of Tomorrow program. Was that a valuable program to your in your career? How?"

EXAMPLE 3:

Fact About Contact (Observation):
You wrote an excellent article about executive coaching.

Follow-Up Question (Related Question):
Do you have preferred coaching resources? Who?

Full Approach:

"I loved your article about executive coaching. Do you have preferred coaching resources? Who?"

YOUR TURN—QUESTIONS 1–3

Observation: _____

Related Question: _____

Observation: _____

Related Question: _____

Observation: _____

Related Question: _____

QUESTION 4: OTHER CONTACTS

You can use the following question exactly as written, or modify it slightly to your style. No matter how you phrase it, you must ask for additional referrals.

"Is there someone else you might refer me to who could be helpful in my job search?"

Your Turn — Question 4 _____

QUESTION 5: HOW CAN I HELP *YOU*?

Again, you can use the following question exactly as written, or modify it slightly to your style. No matter how you phrase it, you must ask how you can help in return.

Your Turn — Question 5 _____

The Great Follow-Up Tracker

WHAT TO DO

Take twenty minutes to follow up after each networking meeting. Here are the steps, laid out for you.

Contact name _____

Business _____

Date _____

FOLLOW UP WITH THE NETWORKING CONTACT

1. Send a brief thank-you to the networking contact.
   ☐ Done
2. Send a brief thank-you to the person who referred you to that contact.
   ☐ Done
3. Add any new or updated information about this person to your networking database.
   ☐ Done
4. Make a note to follow up with this contact, as appropriate.
   ☐ Done

FOLLOW UP WITH YOURSELF

1. What did you do well?_____

_____

2. What will you do differently next time? _____

_____

_____

_____

_____

_____

3. What did you learn and how will you apply that
   information?

_____

_____

_____

_____

FOLLOW UP WITH NEW CONTACTS

1. What names of future contacts did you get?

_____

_____

_____

2. Schedule follow-up with each of these new contacts.
   ☐ Done

About the Authors

MARCIA BALLINGER is a Co-Founder and Principal at Ballinger|Leafblad, a St. Paul-based executive search firm focused on serving the civic sector. She conducts executive search projects for top executives in non-profit organizations, higher education, foundations and professional associations. A frequent presenter to groups of executives, Marcia is widely known as a no-nonsense representative of the executive search industry.

Marcia has a BS in Business Administration and an MA in Speech-Communication along with a PhD in Organization and Management from Capella University where she now serves on the Board of Directors. She was named an Industry Leader by the Minneapolis/St. Paul Business Journal in 2008.

A resident of St. Paul, Marcia lives with her husband Brad, daughter Analisa and their two French Bulldogs. She is at work on a new book focused on job interviewing skills.

You can get in touch with Marcia at www.ballingerleafblad. com.

NATHAN A. PEREZ is Principal at 20-Minute Communications, LLC., a consultancy that helps all experience levels of job-seekers from across the country. He is a national speaker on the topics of networking, résumé deconstruction, and LinkedIn.

As part of his 20-Minute Communications consultancy, Nathan continues to work in executive search in the Research function. Responsible for the first step in the executive recruitment process, Nathan devises the strategies of "where and how to find" qualified candidates for client companies. He has been cited by *The Huffington Post* as one of the most connected people on LinkedIn world-wide.

Co-author of the acclaimed job-search networking book *The 20-Minute Networking Meeting,* Nathan teaches its 5 principles to students, career coaches and executives. An enthusiastic and hands-on coach, Nathan helps strengthen the presence of his job-searching clients by combining his executive search experience with 20 years in front of television cameras and stage performance.

A formally trained actor, Nathan spent 20 years in New York City and Hollywood as a professional performer and writer. He is a member of the Actors Equity Association union (AEA), and a voting union member of The Screen-Actors Guild (SAG-AFTRA).

Nathan is a Bachelor of Fine Arts graduate from the University of Oklahoma, and proudly serves as Board Secretary at The Loft Literary Center, the nation's largest writing institutions dedicated to cultivating creative writers and their work. He lives in Minneapolis with his wife and two kids. You can get in touch or read more about him at www.20mnm.com.

Congratulations—
you've learned to network.
Now go get that job!

Made in the USA
Middletown, DE
31 August 2018